PARIS

A Collection of the Poetry of Place

Edited by
HETTY MEYRIC HUGHES

ELAND • LONDON

This edition first published in April 2014 by Eland Publishing Ltd,
61 Exmouth Market, Clerkenwell, London EC1R 4QL

All poems are copyright © of the authors and translators, as
attributed in the text and in the acknowledgements

This arrangement and commentary © Hetty Meyric Hughes 2014

ISBN 978 1 906011 31 4

Pages designed and typeset by Antony Gray
Cover image: *Le Quai Conti, Paris*, 1896 (oil on canvas) by
Maximilien Luce (1858–1941)
from a Private Collection/Bridgeman Art Library
Printed and bound in Spain by GraphyCems, Navarra

For Otto and Agnes

Contents

Des villes, et encore des villes;
J'ai des souvenirs de villes comme on a des souvenirs d'amour:
A quoi bon en parler? Il m'arrive parfois,
La nuit, de rêver que je suis là, ou bien là,
Et au matin je m'éveille avec un désir de voyage.

Valéry Larbaud (1881–1957)

THE STREETS OF PARIS

Paris has always been an intoxicating cocktail of turbulence and romance, and its poetry exposes this perfectly. It fuses the personal and the political and carries its people on a tide of heroism, engagement and enchantment. The poetry of Paris has always been very committed, rooted in the city's struggles for freedom and equality. As Louis Aragon wrote, 'Nothing has the sparkle of Paris ignited.'

Various *quartiers* of the city have been closely associated with artists and poets, and familiar names conjure forth ghosts of wild parties, poor poets in garrets and bohemian writers.

The Rive Gauche of Paris covers several literary quarters, including Saint-Germain des Prés – dear to the Existentialists – the Latin Quarter famous for its students, and Montparnasse, erstwhile Mecca of artists.

In the 1870s, poets including Verlaine and the Parnassians lived in Montparnasse. Théodore de Banville lived at 26 Rue de Condé (once the residence of Beaumarchais, author of *The Barber of Seville*) and held a Thursday evening salon throughout the 1860s, attended by Verlaine and Mallarmé as well as by the Parnassians. Artists such as Modigliani then arrived, and the great Apollinaire. They were followed by Lenin, Trostsky, Gertrude Stein; then, after World War I, writers and artists migrated to Montparnasse from all over the world. Pablo Neruda wrote,

Paris, France, Europe, for us small-town Bohemians from South America, consisted of a stretch of two hundred meters and a couple of street corners: Montparnasse, La Rotonde, Le Dôme, La Coupole, and three or four other cafes.

Americans in particular were drawn to Montparnasse, and the exchange rate could transform them overnight from destitute to rich enough to party and drink with gay abandon. Many of them stayed on. As Oscar Wilde wrote, 'They say that when good Americans die they go to Paris.'

The area between what is now the Musée Cluny and the river was a cluster of very old squalid streets where students of the Middle Ages studied and took lodgings: among them Dante himself, who refers to the Rue de Fouarre (or straw, on which, following the instructions of Pope Urban V, the students sat) as the 'Vico degli Strami'. It was in the Rue de Bièvre (in a house that no longer stands) that he wrote part of the *Divine Comedy*.

Another more rural area that drew the poets and artists to its heart was Montmartre. Nerval wrote of it in *La Bohème galante* of 1855:

> Here there are windmills, cabarets, rustic pleasances, quiet little streets lined with cottages, farms and half-wild gardens, meadows diversified with miniature precipices and springs gushing from clayey soil, oases of verdure in which goats frolic under the watchful eye of the little girls, sure-footed as mountaineers, who mind them.

As Paris grows and its cultural boundaries expand, so does its poetry, living evidence that perhaps more than any other city in the world, Paris is the crucible of great poetry, inspiring writers and singers, cocooning them and providing the ideal stage for their work.

Poets have always made good flâneurs, fine observers of human life, down to its smallest and most revealing details. The poems that follow all show this sense of poetry arising from its surroundings, inseparable from the very paving stones of the city.

FROM *The Journals of Sylvia Plath*

Friday, March 30 [1956]

A strange day passing through ecstasy unto certain sorrow and the raining of questions sad and lonely on the dark rooftops. Met Gary early & walked to Pont Royal, where I met Tony, feeling very chic in my white pleated skirt and aqua sweater & red shoes & red & white polka-dotted hair-scarf; *citronnade* at kiosque and he was gay and quite sweet; a little more subdued with his sister gone; we took the metro to Pigalle and got out in the hot sun by the honky-tonk square and began climbing the little narrow roads to the top of Montmartre; the shops were dark stenchful holes and reeked of garlic and cheap tobacco. In the sun there was a magic of decay: scabbed pastel posters, leprous umber walls, flowers sprouting out of the filth. Climbed Rue Vieuville & series of steeply angled steps to Place du Tertre, which was chock full of tourists and bad bad artists in various stances doing charcoal portraits or muddy paintings of the domes of Sacré-Cœur; Tony and I walked about and looked at paintings until a small man asked if he could cut my silhouette *'comme un cadeau,'* so I stood in the middle of the square in the middle of Montmartre and gazed at the brilliant restaurants in the middle of a gathering crowd which ohed and ahed and which was just what the little man wanted – to attract customers: so I got a free silhouette and by this time Tony was putting his arm around my waist when we walked and I could feel that bristling barbed wit mellowing: we stood in front of Sacré-Cœur in the sun watching the tourist buses grunt up the hill, full of deadpan people sheltered by sunproof-windproof-bulletproof-glass domes; inside the church it was cool and dark as a well with red patches of light from the windows: Tony described Chartres a bit and some rather gratifying sensitivity came out. Had exquisite lunch just off commercial square where they were serving mobs under the trees and playing violin-lilty tunes, where the man with the picture frame and paper flowers around his head was yelling and doing stunts. We avoided all this in the shady grove of the peaceful Auberge du Coucou and had fine *salade de tomate*, delectable *veau* sautéed in mushrooms and buttery potatoes and bottle of iced white wine which sent us floating into the afternoon like birds, all airy and gay; Tony bought me a bunch of violets and was increasingly attentive and I mellowed to fondness.

and

6 March 1956

I was struck, [even in a tedious session in a dark cubicle in Newham with Miss Barrett lisping sweetly to those immature girls performing an autopsy on *Les Fleurs du Mal*] that I could translate Baudelaire by sight, almost immediately, except for the obvious vocabulary words I didn't know: I felt the sensuous flow of the words and meanings, and plunged in them alone, longing to read him and live with him. Maybe someday French will actually be natural to me . . .

Blanche (Paris)
by Robert Cole (2001)

Petrified orchids at the mouth
    Of the metro Blanche,
    The erotic museum overspilling.
    Everyone from here to Pigalle
    Becomes an exhibit.
The cous cous eaters
    Spooning semolina
    Into their soup,
    The line of mutton bone
    Delicate as the neck of a prostitute.
We watch the long striptease
    Of light washing pavements,
    The X-ray dresses,
    Windows pixilated ghosts,
    Window dressers pimping mannequins.
And an old cleric
    Fresh from the peepshow
    And confessional
    Moves through the Stations of the Cross
    Pursued by his naked congregation.

Robert Cole lives in Brittany and edits *Chimera* magazine.

In the Street

by Jules Laforgue, translated by Peter Dale

The pavement with its trees stunted and thin;
The pregnant women and the bawdy males;
Complaints an inconsolable organ wails;
The cabs, the dailies, adverts, all the din.

Past café fronts where gaunt men ponder in
Their absinthe, gaze blank and mute as veils,
File herds of whores with painted lips and nails,
Hiking up dismal houri tits and skin.

And Earth in vast steppes forever mired,
Forever, and when a thousand years have flown
Paris will be a waste of herds unknown.

And still you'll muse, oh chaste stars, untired:
You island Earth, be gone with a far lob,
Forever rolling, heaving your old sob.

Jules Laforgue moved to Paris from his native Montevideo in 1876
at the age of sixteen. At the end of his life he spent five years in
Berlin, where he wrote much of his best poetry, and died in 1886.
One of the first poets to write in free verse, he was a major influence
on Ezra Pound and T. S. Eliot.

FROM *Zone*

by Guillaume Apollinaire,
from *Alcools* (1913),
translated by Samuel Beckett

This morning I saw a pretty street whose name is gone
Clean and shining clarion of the sun
Where from Monday morning to Saturday evening four
times a day
Directors workers and beautiful shorthand typists go their way
And thrice in the morning the siren makes its moan
And a bell bays savagely coming up to noon
The inscriptions on walls and signs
The notices and plates squawk parrot-wise
I love the grace of this industrial street
In Paris between the Avenue des Ternes and the Rue
Aumont-Thiéville

Also in this poem Apollinaire wrote:

You are tired at last of this old world

O shepherd Eiffel Tower the flock of bridges bleats at the morning

You have had enough of this Greek and Roman antiquity

Urban Renewal

by Raymond Queneau,
from *Pounding the Pavements* (1968),
translated by Teo Savory

With the latest developments
(and those to come)
of modern science and industry
we could easily move
historical monuments
and places of popular entertainment
and put them all together in one
suitably slum-cleared
spot:
Sacré Cœur and Place Pigalle
Eiffel Tower and Sainte-Chapelle
Moulin Rouge and the Halls
of Justice the bookstalls
on the Left Bank rue de Rivoli
and the basins in the Tuileries
the Velodrome and the Opera
   etcetera etcetera
preventing tourists
from spreading out all over the city and
adding to our traffic problems

Carefully Placed

by Raymond Queneau,
translated by William Alwyn

Carefully placed and nicely chosen
it takes a few words to make a poem
words are all right if one loves 'em
in writing a poem
when a poem is born one isn't alway
sperfectly sure what one's trying to say
so it's vital then to look for a theme
to give it a title
at other times one laughs and cries
when writing with poetic lic-
ence there's always something extreme
about a poem

Sunflower

for Pierre Reverdy,
by André Breton (1923),
translated by Mark Polizzotti

The traveler who crossed Les Halles at summer's end
Walked on tiptoe
Despair rolled its great handsome lilies across the sky
And in her handbag was my dream that flask of salts
That only God's godmother had breathed
Torpors unfurled like mist
At the Chien qui Fume
Where pro and con had just entered
They could hardly see the young woman and then only
　　　at an angle
Was I dealing with the ambassadress of salpeter
Or with the white curve on black background we call thought
The Innocents' Ball was in full swing
The Chinese lanterns slowly caught fire in chestnut trees
The shadowless lady knelt on the Pont-au-Change
on Rue Gît-le-Coeur the stamps had changed
The night's promises had been kept at last
The carrier pigeons and emergency kisses
Merged with the beautiful stranger's breasts
Jutting beneath the crepe of perfect meanings
A farm prospered in the heart of Paris
And its windows looked out on the Milky Way
But no one lived there yet because of the guests
Guests who are known to be more faithful than ghosts
Some like that woman appear to be swimming
And a bit of their substance becomes part of love

She internalizes them
I am the plaything of no sensory power
And yet the cricket who sang in hair of ash
One evening near the statue of Etienne Marcel
Threw me a knowing glance
André Breton it said pass

A few notes: the title of this poem, 'Tournesol', means sunflower but also litmus paper. This poem is set around Les Halles, the great market that featured in many novels and poems before being destroyed in the early 1970s and replaced by the current shopping, cinema and swimming pool complex. Le Chien qui Fume was a famous cafe near Les Halles. André Breton met Jacqueline Lamba in 1934 and then considered this poem to have been an extraordinary prefiguration of that encounter. The poem is dedicated to Pierre Reverdy (1889–1960), whom Breton, Aragon and Soupault regarded as 'the greatest poet at present living'. Here are a few lines of his, to give a flavour of his work; the poem is entitled 'The roof slates' (translated by Patricia Terry).

On every slate
                sliding from the roof
                                someone
                    had written
                                    a poem

The gutter is rimmed with diamonds
                                the birds drink them

FROM *Zone*

by Guillaume Apollinaire (1913),
translated by Samuel Beckett

Weeping you watch the wretched emigrants
They believe in God they pray the women suckle their infants
They fill with their smell the station of Saint-Lazare
Like the wise men from the east they have faith in their star
They hope to prosper in the Argentine
And to come home having made their fortune
A family transports a red eiderdown as you your heart
An eiderdown as unreal as our dreams
Some go no further doss in the stews
Of the Rue des Rosiers or the Rue des Ecouffes
Often in the streets I have seen them in the gloaming
Taking the air and like chessmen seldom moving
They are mostly Jews their wives wear wigs and in
The depths of shadowy dens bloodless sit on and on

Notre-Dame de Paris

by Gérard de Nerval (1834),
translated by Olivia McCannon

Notre-Dame is so old – perhaps one day she'll bury
This Paris she's watched spring to life. But
In thousands of years, as a wolf floors cattle,
Time will unfoot this great carcass, bend
Its steel nerves, and then dully and sadly
Set about gnawing its old stone bones.

People from everywhere over the world
Will come to gaze at this austere ruin.
Reading Victor's book and deep in thought
They'll think they can see the old basilica
Just as it was, magnificent, powerful,
Rise up before them like a dead man's shade.

Gérard de Nerval was born in Paris in 1808. He was hailed as a precursor of surrealism by André Breton, and Proust acknowledged his debt to him. According to another poet, Théophile Gautier, Nerval would walk a live lobster on a blue ribbon through the gardens of the Palais-Royal. 'I like lobsters,' he said, 'because they are calm, serious, and know the secrets of the sea.' He suffered from depression, spending several spells in mental health clinics; he was released from the last one after a campaign was mounted by the Société de Gens de Lettres in October 1854 but hanged himself three months later on a snowy winter's evening in 1855. He'd left a note for the aunt with whom he'd been staying: 'Don't wait for me this evening, because the night will be black and white.'

Notre Dame

by Osip Mandelstam, from *Stone*,
translated by Robert Tracy

Where a Roman judge framed laws for an alien folk
A basilica stands, original, exulting,
Each nerve stretched taut along the light cross-vaulting,
Each muscle flexing, like Adam when he first woke.

If you look from outside you grasp the hidden plan:
Strong saddle-girth arches watchfully forestall
The ponderous mass from shattering the wall
And hold in check the bold vault's battering ram.

A primal labyrinth, a wood past men's understanding,
The Gothic sprit's rational abyss,
Brute strength of Egypt and a Christian meekness,
Thin reed beside oak, and the plumb line everywhere king.

Stronghold of Notre Dame, the more my attentive eyes
Studied your gigantic ribs and frame
Then the more often this reflection came:
From cruel weight, I too will someday make beauty rise.

1912

According to his translator, for Mandelstam, stone (also the title of his first collection) was 'the basic building material, just as the word is the basic building material for a poem, and he saw himself not as a creator but as a builder'. He kept his feet firmly on the ground and resisted the Russian Symbolists' mysticism; he was a craftsman rather than a seer. He quoted Villon with approval: 'I know well that I am not the son of an angel, crowned with a diadem from some star or from another planet', adding 'a denial like that is worth the same as a positive assertion'.

Pont des Arts

by Jacques Réda,
from *Retour au calme* (1989),
translated by Olivia McCannon

To my left, the city, once a maze of stone
Is now a flimsy monument of dust or ash
Soundlessly dissolving under pressure from the fog
Then showing up again, ahead – the way a dream does
In a sick man's jostled sleep, ever blurrier –
Between the long reaching hands of the bridges.

And I keep walking, among other shapes that are falling apart,
Through the snow on the quays, towards gardens without end.

Jacques Réda was born in Lorraine in 1929 and moved to Paris as
a young man, and has stayed there and written about it ever since.
The success of his *Ruins of Paris* (1977) established him as a great
poet of the city, a perambulating lyricist who carries a camera
wherever he wanders. He founded *Jazz Magazine* and was the
editor in chief of the *Nouvelle Revue Française*, the literary magazine
created by Andé Gide. This is from his *Ruins of Paris*, translated by
Mark Treharne:

Somehow or other I eventually reach the Place de la Concorde.
Space suddenly becomes maritime. Even with almost no wind
there is a whiff of weighing anchors in the air. And, against the
columns, below the balustrades guarded by lions, the swaying
sailing vessels of a Claude painting surge up, the timber of their
hulls and masts, the rigging, the canvas whistling and creaking,
tearing the smoky flag that is for ever unfurling above the city.
So I walk along as if I were on a beach, through this fallow land.

And perhaps it is the uncertain evening light that opens up such a perspective to my eyes, though it remains merged with the stone and the din of Paris. For in broad daylight, especially during the badly tamed months (February, March, November), when the air pales as it does on the fringes of heathland and marshes, the streets cut through the glow of a sandy estuary; with every step you take a pearly shimmer is on the point of rising up between the dunes, the heart jumps, and whole forests in transhumance park themselves at crossroads then slip out of sight in a single leap, like the unicorn. An elemental yet soothing natural wildness has survived on these monuments. Taking refuge in the sky, the most sensitive part of this world still, it affects even marble, which is impervious to time and season.

Jacques Roubaud (born 1932) is an indefatigable walker and composes his poems with his feet, as he said, 'silently in my head walking'. He is a member of OuLiPo, recruited to it by Raymond Queneau. The group – a 'workshop of potential literature' – still meets on Thursdays. They have created a series of playful, often complex and mathematical constraints, which they use to trigger creativity, in prose (Perec's novel that excludes all instances of the letter 'e', for example) as well as in verse. This poem is from Roubaud's collection of Paris poems of 1999, whose title is taken from Baudelaire's poem 'The Swan'.

Arrondissements

from *The Form of a City Changes Faster, Alas, than
the Human Heart* by Jacques Roubaud,
translated by Keith and Rosmarie Waldrop

In Paris there are twenty arrondissements
There are also 'three-or-four hundred lassies'
According to the song
If 'three hundred' it's fifteen per arrondissement
If 'four hundred' they average twenty
In any case not many
And I have never seen them 'dance among the grassies'.

The twenty arrondissements of Paris are numbered
No 1 is called the Ist Arrondissement
No 2 is called the IInd,
And so on (up to twenty).

In the Ist arrondissement is the main post office in Rue du Louvre.
You can mail your letters there; even on Sunday. That is very
convenient.

The IInd arrondissement is remarkable because it houses (and
will at least till 1998) the Bibliothèque Nationale.

In the IIIrd arrondissement you will find 'the verdant Square des
Arts et des Métiers'. A character in the novel *Les copains* by M.
Farigoule (alias Jules Romain) announces that he is about to go
there 'on the gadget that accelerates the feet'.

The IVth arrondissement is known for the BHV department store.

The Vth arrondissement for its Panthéon, 'a jewel of Gothic art'.

Of the VIth we'll remember the Luxembourg Gardens and its
statues. Raymond Queneau has drawn up a quasi exhaustive list of
them in *Courir les rues* (a book of poems by that author).

The VIIth is towered over by the Eiffel Tower.

The VIIIth by the Arc de Triomphe.

In the IXth is the present residence of M. Roubaud who is composing the present prose poem.

The Xth arrondissement is cut though by the Canal Saint-Martin where once was the Hôtel du Nord whose famous 'atmosphere' we know. It is also here that Louis Jouvet made, to my mind no less famously, this definitive statement: '*Les mères de famille vous disent "mère . . . de famille"*.'

The XIth arrondissement is not the location of the CHU Saint-Antoine Hospital where Georges Perec worked.

This CHU is in the XIIth (if I'm not mistaken; in which case it's *vice versa* or *Lycée de Versailles* as Pierre Dac used to say [unless it was Francis Blanche]).

In the XIIIth I'd point out the Parc Montsouris and its eastern boundary, the Rue Gazan where François Caradec of the Oulipo lives.

The XIVth has the street of la Tombe-Issoire, but not the street of la Folie-Méricourt (which is in the XIth).

The XVth is far, very far. In its Rue des Favorites is the Center for Postal Money Orders.

The XVIth arrondissement has Pomp. Rue de la.

Entering the XVIIth one thinks of Aristide Bruant and his song (I quote from memory, poorly) 'La morale de cette histoir' là / d'cette histoir' là / c'est que les filles qu'a pas d'papa / qu'a pas d'papa 'faut pas les envoyer à l'école / aux Batignolles.'

The XVIIIth is the Butte.

The XIXth is feeling for nature (at the Buttes-Chaumont, obviously).

And now we finally get to the XXth arrondissement. We go to the Mur des Fédérés (not many visitors).

The entire surface of Paris is parceled out among the twenty arrondissements. Not an inch escapes them.

Each arrondissement of Paris is a compact space. One can walk continuously from one point of an arrondissement to another without ever leaving it.

Certain pairs of arrondissements share a border: the Ist borders the IInd, the IInd borders the IIIrd, etc.

Whenever one crosses the border of one arrondissement to go into another one always feels a little thrill: thus M. Roubaud whenever he crossed the Rue d'Amsterdam where he lives. Because the side with uneven numbers is in the VIIIth, and not in the IXth (which the post office will take upon itself to remind you of by stamping a letter addressed to M. Roubaud in the VIIIth with a severe 'wrong address, letter delayed'). But where exactly is the border? Is it a narrow band that runs the whole length of the street?

The most remarkable spots of Paris are those where several arrondissements meet: thus on Place de l'Etoile the VIIIth, XVIth and XVIIth. The crossroad of Boulevard de Belleville, Rue de Belleville, Rue du Faubourg-du-Temple and the Boulevard de la Villette belongs by right to four arrondissements: the Xth, XIth XIXth and XXth. There are other examples that you can make your own list of.

Four and no more than four colors are sufficient to color the map of Paris in such a way that no two adjacent arrondissements are of the same color.

Between the XVth and XVIth, under the Pont Mirabeau, flows the Seine.

Roubaud's last line refers to what is perhaps the most famous French poem about Paris. So without further ado, here it is, translated by the poet Olivia McCannon, a resident of the Belleville area of Paris and whose own verse is steeped in the city.

Pont Mirabeau
by Guillaume Apollinaire

Under Pont Mirabeau flows the Seine
Along with our love
Must I be reminded again
Joy only ever came after pain

Night will come the hour will strike
Days go by while I remain

Hand in hand we'll stay face to face
While under the bridge
Of our arms the lapping waves
Of our looks endlessly interlace.

Night will come the hour will strike
Days go by while I remain

Love goes the way of the water flowing
Love goes
Life is slow
And how harsh Hope

Night will come the hour will strike
Days go by while I remain

Days go by and weeks go by
　　　Neither time past
　　Nor love come again
Under Pont Mirabeau flows the Seine

　　Night will come the hour will strike
　　Days go by while I remain

Born Wilhelm Apollinaris de Kostrowitsky in 1880, the illegitimate son of a Polish woman and an Italian nobleman, Apollinaire grew up in Monaco then moved to Paris as a young man. Here he befriended the artists Picasso, Derain, Braque, Gris, Léger, Picabia, Duchamp. In 1913 he published *Alcools*, one of the most popular books of French poetry ever, and a series of essays celebrating Cubism.

In 1911 Apollinaire was arrested and imprisoned for a few days in La Santé in connection with the *Mona Lisa*, for it had apparently been stolen from the Louvre by Apollinaire's secretary, who, on a previous occasion, had stolen a Phoenician statuette and two other figurines. He had given them to Apollinaire, who in turn gave them to Picasso, who modelled the ears of his *Demoiselles d'Avignon* on them. Apollinaire's innocence was soon proved and the painting returned to the Louvre.

After a thwarted love affair and perhaps to rebuild his reputation after the *Mona Lisa* incident he applied for French citizenship and enlisted in the army. He learned from Futurists and drew poetry from objects such as planes, submarine cables, phones, the phonograph; he also borrowed their technique of *simultanéisme*, or simultaneous narratives. He is said to have coined the term 'Surrealism' to characterise *Parade*, a ballet to which Cocteau, Satie and Picasso had contributed. Surrealism came to represent a higher reality (*la sur-réalité*), beyond the superficial appearances of the everyday.

Apollinaire would place objects in illogical juxtapositions and anticipated what later became the Surrealist movement, partly because of his audacity in breaking from the strict rules of French versification and punctuation. He borrowed technical terms rather than using only veiled or esoteric poetic vocabulary, and bypassed punctuation.

He survived a shell wound to his head and subsequent trepanning but succumbed to the Spanish flu epidemic of 1918, shortly after the publication of the collection of *Calligrammes*, poems of peace and war. Blaise Cendrars wrote of him:

Apollinaire

1900–1911

For twelve years France's only poet

And Cocteau wrote of his work, 'Apollinaire chanted his poems while writing them and they enchant us. These old-fashioned secrets are more worthwhile than Aristotle.'

A STOLEN KISS

Some French expressions have found their natural equivalents in English and vice-versa. To take French leave becomes *filer à l'anglaise*; a French letter is a *capote anglaise*. The French describe a shade of apple green as *vert anglais* while we have Paris green, a vivid, light green pigment manufactured in Paris. The French refer to *boucles anglaises* to describe ringlets while we have French plaits; we might put a French hem or French cuff on a blouse stitched with *broderie anglaise*; an orchestra may have a *cor anglais* or a French horn playing in it. But French kissing has only ever been French.

Il Bacio

by Paul Verlaine, from *Poems Under Saturn* (1866),
translated by Karl Kirchwey

Kiss! Hollyhock in the garden of caresses!
Lively accompaniment on the keyboard of the teeth
To the soft refrains that Love sings in passionate hearts with
Its archangel's voice to enchanting languidness!

Resonant and graceful Kiss, heavenly Kiss!
Nonpareil voluptuousness, intoxication indescribable!
All hail! The man, bent over your adorable
Cup, gets drunk there with an inexhaustible happiness.

As by music, as by a Rhine wine,
You cradle us and we are consoled,

And sorrow expires with a pout in your crimson fold . . .
Let a greater one, Goethe or Will, write you a classic line.

Me, I can't do it, this bouquet of childish strophes
Is all I can offer, a sickly trouvère of Paris:
Be kind and, to reward me, come down on the mischievous
Lips of One I know, Kiss, and laugh.

Paris at Night

by Jacques Prévert,
translated by Sarah Lawson

Three matches lit one by one in the night
The first to see your whole face
The second to see your eyes
The last to see your mouth
And complete darkness to remind me of all that
As I hold you in my arms.

Jacques Prévert (1900–1977) was an immensely popular poet, songwriter and screenwriter, author of *Les Enfants du Paradis*. He is loved by children for his playful poems about school. During the German occupation some of his poems were censored, such as the song 'Barbara', and enjoyed a great success. He never considered himself a poet but has had schools and a Paris street (in the 20th *arrondissement*) named after him.

The Garden

by Jacques Prévert,
translated by Sarah Lawson

Thousands and thousands of years
               Would not be enough
                              To express
               The little second of eternity
                        When you kissed me
                              When I kissed you
One morning in the slight winter light
In the half dark Montsouris Park in Paris
                              In Paris
                        On the Earth
               The Earth which is a star.

Paris First Named

by Jacques Brel (1961), translated by Olivia McCannon

As the sun starts to rise
And the rooftops shine
Paris alight
As the Seine goes its way
And points me towards mine
Paris a sign
As my heart skips a beat
At your heart as it smiles
Paris hello
As your hand finds my hand
And we both understand

Paris in love
As we raise our first glass
On the Île Saint-Louis
Paris a wish
As we steal a first kiss
On a bridge in the sun
Paris begun
And the next that we take
By a Tuileries gate
Paris romance
As two heads turn and sigh
At the sight of Versailles
Paris all France

Days that go by
Without counting the hours
Paris desire
Hours where our eyes
See only each other
Paris a mirror
Night draws a line
Beneath songs that we sing
Paris sleep tight
The day comes at last
When the barriers crash
Paris tonight
This small shabby room
Where we end the dance
Paris you and I
A look that soaks up
All the love in the world
Paris your eyes
The vow I sob out when

I can't speak the words
Paris a cry
To know that tomorrow
Will be like today
Paris delight

But the end of the trip
Means the end of the song
Paris grey skies
The last day the last hour
Brings the first tear
Paris overcast
All the flowers have gone
From the gardens we crossed
Paris dull dawn
The station confirms
The departure's at nine
Paris goodbye
Out of mind out of sight
Out of reach paradise
Paris forlorn
But a letter from you
Saying yes and I will
Paris once more
Cities and towns
Pass shining and bright
As you wait for me there
Now our lives are on track
Paris I'm back.

The Belgian Jacques Brel is another name closely associated with
songs and music; he moved to Paris in 1955 but spent most of his
time on tour.

Rose Blanche

by Aristide Bruant

She had, under her marten cape
On the Montmartre Hill
A little innocent air;
She was called Rose, she was beautiful,
smelt of new flowers
Rue St Vincent.

No one knew her father,
She no longer had her mother,
And since 1900,
She stayed with her old grandma
Where she grew up, like that, alone,
Rue St Vincent.

She worked, already, to live,
And on the frosty eves
In the dark freezing cold
Her little scarf on her shoulders
She went home, via the Rue des Saules,
Rue St Vincent.

She saw, in the freezing nights,
The starry sky
And the crescent moon,
That glowed, white and fateful
On the little cross of the basilica,
Rue St Vincent.

In summer, during the warm dusks,
She met Jules
Who was so sensual

She stayed, the whole evening,
With him, near the old cemetery,
Rue St Vincent.

But little Jules was a pimp,
So, the adolescent,
Seeing she didn't go with the gang,
Thrust his knife in her belly,
Rue St Vincent.

When they covered the coffin,
She was all white
When they were burying her,
The undertakers said that the poor kid
Was killed on her wedding day
Rue St Vincent.

She had, under her marten cape
On the Montmartre Hill
A little innocent air;
She was called Rose, she was beautiful,
smelt of new flowers
Rue St Vincent.

Aristide Bruant was the great *chansonnier* of the cabarets of Montmartre in the 1880s and 1890s, and it was reported that he sung his poetry with 'the most cutting voice, the most metallic voice I have ever heard; a voice of rioting and the barricades . . . an arrogant and brutal voice which penetrated your soul like the stab of a switchblade into a straw man'.

A Paris Love-Affair

by Armen Lubin,
translated by Graham Dunstan Martin

The year of my first, my greatest love
Was the year of the luminous clocks.
It was the year they stood at every crossroad
With a big fire inside
And Paris was one radiant brightness,
A brightness I deserved.

Afterwards it rained three days out of three,
We walked in the wet dark
We walked, walked by the Seine
but if there are hours I remember
They are those incised within me
In black on legendary white
In black beyond description.

Armen Lubin (1903–1974) was of Armenian origin; he fled from Turkey and genocide, moving to Paris in 1923. He was already an established novelist in Armenian before starting to write in French in 1945.

Paris

by Arthur Symons (1894)

My Paris is a land where twilight days
Merge into violent nights of black and gold;
Where, it may be, the flower of dawn is cold:
Ah, but the gold nights, and the scented ways!

Eyelids of women, little curls of hair,
A little nose curved softly, like a shell,
A red mouth like a wound, a mocking veil:
Phantoms, before the dawn, how phantom-fair!

And every woman with beseeching eyes,
Or with enticing eyes, or amorous,
Offers herself, a rose, and craves of us
A rose's place among our memories.

Arthur Symons was a poet and critic, and translated the works
of the French Symbolists, introducing the poetry of Laforgue to
T. S. Eliot.

Ballade of the Girls of Paris

by François Villon, from *The Testament* (c.1461),
translated by H. B. McCaskie

The Florence girls can talk a bit,
  The Venice girls no less than these,
Even the old ones, I admit,
  Are fit to carry messages:
  But Lombard girls or Genevese
Or Roman (I'll stake all I've got)
  Or Savoyard or Piedmontese,
The Paris girls out-talk the lot.

The Naples girls hold Chairs of Wit,
  So people say, and give degrees:
A German or a Prussian chit
  Can prattle with a certain ease:
  But take girls anywhere you please,
Hungarian, Greek or Gipsy trot,
  Castilian or Aragonese,
The Paris girls out-talk the lot.

Swiss, Bretons have no skill in it,
  Nor Toulouse girls nor Gasconese,
Two P'tit Pont fishwives would be fit
  To bring them crying to their knees:
  Are these enough geographies?
Take the Lorrainers, English, Scot,
  The Calais girls, the Picardese,
The Paris girls out-talk the lot.

Prince, give the prize for subtleties
  Of speech to Paris: heed it not

If rumour says the Italians please,
The Paris girls out-talk the lot.

In his biography of Villon, Wyndham Lewis describes him in harsh terms (less so his verse):

He was as weak as water, as variable as a weather-cock, mercurial, impulsive, idle, mocking, childlike, egoistic, warm-hearted, sensual, careless, driven before every gust of desire; a rake and a spendthrift worshipping beauty; a common criminal firm in faith and affection; a companion of thieves and whores and vagabonds, producing from the dregs of his life an exquisite flower of pure poetry; a temper as flecked with dark and light as an April day. Above all, melancholy possessed him soon, whether his mood was gaiety, or defiance, or recollection.

NOSTALGIA, LONGING AND EXILE

Many poems about Paris share a common theme of nostalgia, the 'ubi sunt' sentiment made famous by François Villon in this poem:

The Ballad of Dead Ladies
by Dante Gabriel Rossetti,
from *Three Translations from François Villon, 1450*
(first published 1870)

Tell me now in what hidden way is
Lady Flora the lovely Roman?
Where's Hipparchia, and where is Thais,
Neither of them the fairer woman?
Where is Echo, beheld of no man,
Only heard on river and mere, –
She whose beauty was more than human? . . .
But where are the snows of yester-year?

Where's Héloise, the learned nun,
For whose sake Abeillard, I ween,
Lost manhood and put priesthood on?
(From Love he won such dule and teen!)
And where, I pray you, is the Queen
Who willed that Buridan should steer
Sewed in a sack's mouth down the Seine? . . .
But where are the snows of yester-year?

White Queen Blanche, like a queen of lilies,
With a voice like any mermaiden –
Bertha Broadfoot, Beatrice, Alice,
And Ermengarde the lady of Maine, –
And that good Joan whom Englishmen
At Rouen doomed and burned her there, –
Mother of God, where are they then? . . .
But where are the snows of yester-year?

Nay, never ask this week, fair lord,
Where they are gone, nor yet this year,
Except with this for an overword, –
But where are the snows of yester-year?

Here's another lament by Villon, a less lofty one this time. It shows his delight in carnal, seamy city life and the melancholy admission of mortality, delivered with gusto and probably from a prison cell. As Hilaire Belloc wrote of Villon, 'If you desire one word to use as an antithesis to the word sentimental, use the word Villon.'

The Lament of the Gorgeous Helmet-Fettler
by François Villon, from *The Testament* (c.1461),
translated by Jane Tozer

'You should have seen my bright unwrinkled brow
The tumbling golden locks. I'd toss my head
And give one sidelong glance – like this – just so
I'd flash my baby-blues and knock 'em dead.
Had hardened cynics begging me to bed.
That straight and perfect nose – where is it now?
Such dainty ears, my face a cameo
A dimple fit to kiss. Lips coral-red.

'My shoulders, soft and fragile, pleased the eye.
Long shapely arms, fine smooth unblemished hands,
Sweet budding breasts, my haunches firm and high
The loins well-muscled, nifty to withstand
And parry in the joust and thrust of love.
Well-rounded hips, thighs parting to disclose
My pretty little rosy quelque-chose
Hidden inside its fragrant bushy grove.

'Just see me now. Quite broken down, world-weary
A forehead crazed with lines. Hair – hanks of grey.
Once-shapely eyebrows sparse, and eyes grown bleary
That with a look drew moneyed men my way.
This broken nose is not a pretty feature
Nor heavy earlobes tufted with thick moss
A pallid, moribund, pathetic creature
With toothless wizened mouth. Fancy a kiss?

'This way goes human beauty, and all flesh.
Cramped limbs; distorted fingers clenched with pain
Shoulders and back hunched forward in distress
The tits and arse just pitiful remains.
Blotched salami thighs; brittle bones like sticks.
My little wotsit? Huh! You cheeky sod,
Don't even go there, mate. I know your tricks.
Remember – this is how I'll meet my God.

'All huddled up, a bunch of sad old bags
We hunker down to mourn those happier days
Squat on our bum-bones, foul-mouthed mad old hags
Our weedy hemp-stalk fire, no roaring blaze.
We're wisps of wool, a spinner's teased-out rolags.
The fire burns out. The wind blows us away.
We were so lovely, once, us poxed-out slags.
This mortal city. No abiding stay . . . '

More than four centuries later the African–American jazz poet Langston Hughes wrote to the same tune while he was working as a dishwasher in Le Grand Duc nightclub, on the corner of Rue Fontaine and Rue Pigalle:

Parisian Beggar Woman
by Langston Hughes (1927)

Once you were young.
Now, hunched in the cold,
Nobody cares
That you are old.

Once you were beautiful.
Now, in the street,
No one remembers
Your lips were sweet.

Oh, withered old woman
Of rue Fontaine,
Nobody but death
Will kiss you again.

Trip to Paris

by Guillaume Apollinaire,
translated by Roger Shattuck

Ah what a charming ride
To leave a gloomy countryside
    For Paris
Lovely Paris
Which long ago
Love must have found beautified
Ah what a charming ride
To leave a gloomy countryside
For Paris

In Paris

by Jean Follain, from *Usage du temps* (1943),
translated by Olivia McCannon

Rugs shaken at windows
are the most threadbare of signs.
O Paris you cling to a memory of thatch
when all your mistresses
wept and undressed
when all your lovers
wore sewn into their jackets
the tiny stitches of suffering.
A city chained
to the pallor of its women
to the eyes of its poets, to its dives.
On shadowy landings we sense

your stunted plants sprouting
and the coming of age of your little queens
who will drink concoctions
as colourful as the chimera.
O handkerchiefs fluttering at casement windows,
girls fainting away in museums,
Bedrooms smelling of hazelnut and love.

Jean Follain (1903–1971) was a magistrate from Normandy. He resisted lyrical outpourings of sentiment and preferred to offer no comment, using few metaphors but instead vivid, painterly images and surprising juxtapositions. In his poems he evokes the intense sensations that give life value, even after the objects or events that inspired them have disappeared, asking, 'Isn't it the poet's duty to save everything?' In the opening lines of his poem 'Homage to Jean Follain' Gael Turnbull wrote,

I think you must have written them on postcards, your poems,
like something one sends home while visiting abroad;

or like woodcuts that one finds in an old book in the attic and
stares at on a rainy day, forgetting supper, forgetting to
switch on the light;

but not antique, though out of time, each fixed in its moment,
like sycamore seeds spiralling down that never seem to
reach the grass.

Paris Suite: Paris

by André Frénaud,
translated by Olivia McCannon

O sleeping ship
that waits for me
at a distance, o Paris
my honour and my feast,
my secret warmed
in your eyes.

O my Seine stowed
in your spring waters,
o innocent bone-vaults
of memory, o my departed
life turning green,
fuller than your days
when they shine.

O your snow in my soul
and my flowers, o mantle
made to glitter in the winter
of my old age,
my wounds
are the colour of your sky.

O Paris, your arenas
for fighting my beasts,
my bulls washed white
by night and my death
by trampling and my blood
spurting into their eyes
and my laughter.

O Paris, your new-bridges
to cross my depths,
your two islands my eyes
flickering on the floodtide,
your night-lit windows
my remote hopes
and your hotel doors
my way into mystery.

O Montmartre, your prow
and your towers to raise
my refusals, your rose windows
to mirror beauty
and morning markets
and park cries
the tender word of the day.

O Paris, my bitter
blue almond
my pensive reserve,
down to the stones
of your breast
my sweet grasses
your hawkers of colour
trees of my uttering voice
and your spoiling sky
o my enchanted helmet.

André Frénaud (1907–1993) worked most of his life as a civil
servant with the French railway. During the war he joined
the Resistance and wrote verse for Paul Éluard's clandestine
publications. Éluard wrote of him:

Sociability is one of the dominant characteristics of the poetry of André Frénaud . . . it is not a stranger speaking, but my friend André Frénaud. I hear him imagine, put to the test, and confirm the strong words that are the life of others and the militant truth of the poet.

Amphion

by Raymond Queneau, from *The Seyes*,
translated by Teo Savory

The Paris you once loved
is not the one we love
and we go slowly
toward what we'll soon forget

Topographies! Itineraries!
Drifting around town!
Memories fading in outdated diaries!
How difficult is remembrance . . .

Without a map at hand
you'll never understand us
because all this is just a game:
the forgetting of time past.

Raymond Queneau (1903–1976) was an active member of the Surrealist Movement between 1924 and 1930. He worked at the publishing house Gallimard as a reader, then editor, then secretary general. He is most famous in the UK for his novel *Zazie dans le Métro*. He once wrote:

I have set myself (in the novel) rules as strict as those of a sonnet . . . One can rhyme characters and situations as one

rhymes words, one can even be satisfied with alliterations. In
fact, I have never seen essential differences between the novel,
of the kind I want to write, and poetry.

FROM *Prose of the Trans-Siberian and of Little Jeanne of France*
by Blaise Cendrars (1913),
translated by Olivia McCannon

Dedicated to musicians

O Paris
Great warm hearth with the criss-crossing embers of your roads
    and old buildings stooping over to warm themselves like
    aged female relatives
And here, look, posters, red green chequered as my short past
    and yellow
Yellow the jaunty colour of French novels abroad.
I love to brush against moving buses in big cities
The Saint-Germain-Montmartre line carries me off to storm
    the Butte.
Motorcars bellow like golden bulls
The cows of dusk chew the cud of Sacré-Coeur

O Paris
Central station disembarcation point of wishes, crossroads of
    anxieties
A little light still falls on the doors of newspaper-sellers but
    that's all
The International Company of Sleeper and Great European
    Express trains has sent me its brochure

It's the most beautiful church in the world
I have friends who surround me like parapets
Scared that once I'm gone I won't come back
All the women I've ever met loom up on the horizon
Semaphores in the rain with sorrowing gestures and sad faces
Bella, Agnès, Catherine and the mother of my son in Italy
And the other, in America, the mother of my love
I hear siren wails that rip through my soul
Far off in Manchuria a belly tremors again as in labour
I wish
I wish I had never gone travelling
Tonight I'm tormented by a great passion
And despite myself I think of little Jeanne of France.
It was on a night of sadness that I wrote this poem in her
        honour Jeanne
The young prostitute
I feel sad I feel so sad
I'll go to the Lapin Agile to redeem my lost youth
And drink shots of liquor
Then come home alone

Paris
City of the One-and-Only Tower of the great Gallows and
        of the Wheel.

At the age of fifteen Blaise Cendrars left home to work for a jewel
merchant, travelling with him through Russia, Persia and China.
He was later a war correspondent, a music-hall juggler, a farmhand,
a hunter. He met Apollinaire in Paris in 1910 and was profoundly
influenced by him, and soon began writing long poems, of which
this is an extract.

   Cendrars wrote, quoting Villon:

Poetry is in the street. It goes arm in arm with laughter. They take each other for a drink, at the source, in the neighbourhood bistros, where the laughter of the people is so flavoursome and the language which flows from their lips so beautiful. 'Il n'est bon bec que de Paris.'

Earlier in the same poem, he wrote,

> I'm scared
> I don't know how to get to the end
> I could paint a series of mad scenes like my friend Chagall
> But I didn't take notes on my travels
> Forgive my ignorance

Incidentally, the artist Sonia Delaunay illustrated this poem about a journey on the Trans-Siberian Railway by creating a two-metre long book folded like an accordion. She reproduced Cendrars' text vertically, juxtaposed with her own painting of simultaneously contrasting colours and forms. This collaboration, 'the first simultaneous book', merging text and design, triggered a great debate throughout Europe about the nature of simultaneity.

At times the yearnings of nostalgia are expressed poignantly from poets in exile *in* Paris not from it.

Rue du Faubourg du Temple
by Olivia McCannon (2011)

The world in one road –
In it a SNACK with too many chairs
A fridge you might fall into up front
An Aljazeera window on the wall
Where a crowd in flames shakes fists
At the *cervelle d'agneau* you ordered

As the News made you nervous now
You must eat it you're twenty-five
This street these intervening lives
Wallpaper to your own sweet will
You step from the apple tobacco fug
Into the stink of street-horn and shove

The pavement's a pitfall of spit and wheels
Dodge a baby's flung-out arm – now – next
An oil-drum trolley hot with blackened corn
Men washed blue by strip-lit caves where
Teapots footballs phonecards proliferate or
Microwaves ping out soft pork dumplings

This will all never be anything but
The surface of what you'll never know
The vanishing forking wakes of flies
With troubled compasses stop-starting
Across the sheer skin that just holds
Over the depth of time and place.

It seems fitting to end this chapter on nostalgia with the poet who broods best, and whose verse reappears often in later pages of this book:

The Swan

by Charles Baudelaire (1859),
translated by James Huneker

To Victor Hugo

1

Andromache, I think of you! The stream,
The poor, sad mirror where in bygone days
Shone all the majesty of your widowed grief,
The lying Simoïs flooded by your tears,
Made all my fertile memory blossom forth
As I passed by the new-built Carrousel.
Old Paris is no more (a town, alas,
Changes more quickly than man's heart may change);
Yet in my mind I still can see the booths;
The heaps of brick and rough-hewn capitals;
The grass; the stones all over-green with moss;
The *débris*, and the square-set heaps of tiles.

There a menagerie was once outspread;
And there I saw, one morning at the hour
When toil awakes beneath the cold, clear sky,
And the road roars upon the silent air,
A swan who had escaped his cage, and walked
On the dry pavement with his webby feet,
And trailed his spotless plumage on the ground.
And near a waterless stream the piteous swan
Opened his beak, and bathing in the dust
His nervous wings, he cried (his heart the while
Filled with a vision of his own fair lake):
'O water, when then wilt thou come in rain?
Lightning, when wilt thou glitter?'

Sometimes yet
I see the hapless bird – strange, fatal myth –
Like him that Ovid writes of, lifting up
Unto the cruelly blue, ironic heavens,
With stretched, convulsive neck a thirsty face,
As though he sent reproaches up to God!

2

Paris may change; my melancholy is fixed.
New palaces, and scaffoldings, and blocks,
And suburbs old, are symbols all to me
Whose memories are as heavy as a stone.
And so, before the Louvre, to vex my soul,
The image came of my majestic swan
With his mad gestures, foolish and sublime,
As of an exile whom one great desire
Gnaws with no truce. And then I thought of you,
Andromache! torn from your hero's arms;
Beneath the hand of Pyrrhus in his pride;
Bent o'er an empty tomb in ecstasy;
Widow of Hector – wife of Helenus!
And of the negress, wan and phthisical,
Tramping the mud, and with her haggard eyes
Seeking beyond the mighty walls of fog
The absent palm-trees of proud Africa;
Of all who lose that which they never find;
Of all who drink of tears; all whom grey grief
Gives suck to as the kindly wolf gave suck;
Of meagre orphans who like blossoms fade.
And one old Memory like a crying horn
Sounds through the forest where my soul is lost . . .
I think of sailors on some isle forgotten;
Of captives; vanquished . . . and of many more.

PARIS, THE ARTIST'S MUSE

Paris's poets have been influenced by the painters of the city, often inspired by their ideas to propel their own intellectual activity. Artists and poets alike painted the city itself, a source of inspiration and delight, dream, filth, beauty, incubus and fantasy. Far from the idylls of country life and pastoral musings, Paris provided the bricks and mortar for the poetry of Baudelaire and his followers.

Parisian Landscape
by Charles Baudelaire,
translated by Laurence Lerner

I need to live among the roofs and towers
Like an astrologer among his stars,
I need to dream (to write my pastorals)
Through solemn noises from the nearby bells,
And wake, and hear them still; lean out and see
The many-masted city under me,
Paris, my restless workshop: drainpipes, spires,
The endless sky in reach of my desires.

Windows and stars light up among the mist.
I lean and watch, my chin upon my fist,
Rivers of smoke ascend and merge: the pale
And blatant moon is pouring out her spell.
Year in, year out, I'll watch the seasons pass
– Spring summer autumn – staring through the glass,
Till winter spreads its white monotony;
Then close the shutters on my fantasy.

All night in dreams I'll pass through shimmering halls;
Fountains will weep from alabaster bowls,
Birds sing and lovers kiss beneath blue skies,
The sound of flutes makes palaces arise.
Winter can riot at the window pane,
I shall not lift my head, or hear the rain,
Drowned in the damp voluptuous atmosphere
Through which my childhood idylls reappear,
In which the sun that sets my thoughts on fire
Charges the heavy climate with desire.

The poet who is virtually synonymous with Paris, the beacon not only of his generation and nation but of all poetry after him, led a rather disenchanted life. As Sartre wrote,

> 'He didn't get the life he deserved.' Baudelaire's life seems a splendid illustration of this comforting maxim. He certainly didn't deserve his mother, constant financial troubles, a board of guardians, his skinflint mistress nor syphilis.

He was also punished for being so ahead of his times, and the court case of *Les Fleurs du Mal* in 1857, on charges of offending religious morality (acquitted) and of offending public morality (condemned, on the basis of the sordid realism of his poetry), caused a scandal at least as great as the *Madame Bovary* case a little earlier. Baudelaire and his publisher were fined for offending against public morals, and ordered to remove six poems from the collection. A reviewer in *Le Figaro* cast doubt on the poet's sanity and called the collection 'a hospital open to all the aberrations of the human mind and to all the putrescence of the human heart'. But Baudelaire's great strength is precisely what his critics recoiled at, for 'beauty is always bizarre', as he wrote in an essay of 1855.

Three months after the court case the (rather strait-laced) Goncourt brothers recorded in their journal:

Baudelaire had supper at the table next to ours. He was without a cravat, his shirt open at the neck and his head shaved, just as if he were going to be guillotined. A single affectation: his little hands washed and cared for, the nails kept scrupulously clean. The face of a maniac, a voice that cuts like a knife, and a precise elocution that tries to copy Saint-Just and succeeds. He denies, with some obstinacy and a certain harsh anger, that he has offended morality with his verse.

This poem and the next (The Sun) are from his 'Tableaux parisiens' in *Les Fleurs du Mal*, an attempt by the poet to re-establish contact with the world of common experience, to escape from the self (through retreating into his garret, ironically). Baudelaire lived through the total transformation of Paris, as Haussmann flattened the medieval quarters and created parks, railway stations, monuments and army-sized boulevards, so much of the city was a building site while he lived here.

The Sun
by Charles Baudelaire,
translated by Olivia McCannon

Along the old quarter, where shutters
Hang from hovels, harbouring secret lusts
When the harsh sun beats down still harder
On the city and the fields, the roofs and the wheat,
I practise my imaginary fencing, alone,
Sniffing out from corners happy rhymes,
Tripping over words as I might paving-stones,
At times bumping into some long-dreamed-of line,

This nurturing father, enemy of chlorosis,
Rouses in the fields both verse-worms and roses;
He makes troubles evaporate into air,
Sets honey flowing in hives and brains
And gives hobbled men their youth back again,
Turning them sweet and carefree as young girls.
He commands the harvest to ripen and shower
Into the undying heart its requirement of flowers.

When, like a poet, he descends into cities
He dignifies all that is mean and shitty
And enters like a king, with no fuss, no valets
Into every asylum, into every palace.

The poet sees himself leaving his attic and going into the city to
record his impressions, transforming what he sees into something
unique. Baudelaire's poetry catches it all: the palace and the slums,
the Seine and the streets, sounds and smells as well as sights.

Leading-Lights

by Charles Baudelaire, from *Les Fleurs du Mal*,
translated by Olivia McCannon

Rubens, river of forgetting, garden of sloth,
Pillow of cool flesh where love cannot be,
But where life collects and quivers incessantly,
Like the air in the sky and the sea in the sea ;

Da Vinci, looking glass, dark and deep,
In which sweet angels, their gentle smiles
Weighted with mystery, appear in the shadows
Of the pines and peaks that border their country;

Rembrandt, mournful murmuring asylum,
With a single crucifix to redeem its bare walls,
Where a prayer comes sobbing out of the squalor,
Coldly cross-sectioned by some winter beam;

Michaelangelo, shadowland, where Christ-figures
Mingle with Hercules, men tall and looming,
Powerful phantoms, cracking their knuckles
As they rip through their shrouds in the gloaming;

A boxer's rages, a satyr's sauce,
You, who captured the beauty of boors,
Puffed-up proud hearts, flaky weak men,
Puget, gloomy emperor of prisoners;

Watteau, carnival where luminous souls
Come to flicker, flamboyant as butterflies,
In dewy, flimsy decors lit by torches
That spill wild light on whirling dances;

Goya, nightmare full of unknown things,
Of the witching hour when a foetus is stewing,
Of old women in mirrors and naked young girls
That call up your demons by fixing a stocking;

Delacroix, bloodbath haunted by bad angels,
Shaded by evergreen forests of pines
Beneath dejected skies, where weird fanfares
Sound and are gone, like Weber's stifled sighs;

These curses, these laments, these blasphemies,
These sobs, these shrieks, these Te Deums, these ecstasies,
Are one echo ringing off a thousand labyrinth walls;
The divine opium of the hearts of mortals.

> Are a cry taken up by a thousand sentinels,
> An order shouted through a thousand megaphones;
> A beacon that lights up a thousand citadels,
> The call of lost hunters in forests immeasurable.
>
> For this, Lord, is truly the best account
> We might ever give of our dignity –
> This passionate sob, rolling through the ages,
> Dying out on the shores of your eternity.

The qualities which Baudelaire evokes in the stanza which begins 'These curses, these laments, these blasphemies' are the very same notes as give *Les Fleurs du Mal* its special resonance, perhaps the consolation for the transience of mortality. The final exaltation is man's cry up to God, the Infinite, the Eternal, borne upwards by poetry and art.

Paintings by all these masters exist in the Louvre now; in Baudelaire's time he would have seen some in the *Salons* exhibitions, some in the Louvre, or along the Quai Voltaire where reproductions were sold (of Watteau, for example).

The Louvre inspired other poets too. Here James Russell Lowell (1819–1891) writes about the *Mona Lisa*:

> She gave me all that woman can
> Nor her soul's nunnery forego,
> A confidence that man to man
> Without remorse can never show.
>
> Rare art, that can the sense refine
> Till not a pulse rebellious stirs,
> And, since she never can be mine,
> Makes it seem sweeter to be hers!

Walter Savage Landor (1775–1864) wrote lines that could accompany a visit to the museum:

First bring me Raphael, who alone hath seen
In all her purity Heaven's Virgin Queen,
Alone hath felt true beauty; bring me then
Titian, ennobler of the noblest men;
And next the sweet Correggio, nor chastise
His little Cupids for those wicked eyes.
I want not Rubens's pink puffy bloom,
Nor Rembrandt's glimmer in a dirty room
With these, nor Poussin's nymph-frequented woods,
His templed heights and long-drawn solitudes.
I am content, yet fain would look abroad
On one warm sunset of Ausonian Claude.

Another poem to accompany a visit to the Louvre is by Dante
Gabriel Rossetti, composed after he wrote of the painting in a letter
to his brother that it was 'so intensely fine that I condescended to
sit down before it and write a sonnet'.

For a Venetian Pastoral

by Giorgione (in the Louvre)
by Dante Gabriel Rossetti (1881)

Water, for anguish of the solstice: – nay,
But dip the vessel slowly, – nay, but lean
And hark how at its verge the wave sighs in
Reluctant. Hush! beyond all depth away
The heat lies silent at the brink of day:
Now the hand trails upon the viol-string
That sobs, and the brown faces cease to sing,
Sad with the whole of pleasure. Whither stray
Her eyes now, from whose mouth the slim pipes creep

And leave it pouting, while the shadowed grass
Is cool against her naked side? Let be: –
Say nothing now unto her lest she weep,
Nor name this ever. Be it as it was, –
Life touching lips with Immortality.

Finally, a poem from the Nobel Prize winner Derek Walcott, born
in St Lucia in 1930.

FROM *Tiepolo's Hound*
by Derek Walcott (2000)

O, the exclamation of white roses, of a wet
grey day of glazed pavements, the towers

in haze of Notre Dame's silhouette
in the Easter drizzle, lines banked with flowers

and umbrellas flowering, then bobbing like mushrooms
in the soup-steaming fog! Paris looked edible:

salads of parks, a bouillabaisse of fumes
from its steaming trees in the incredible

fragrance of April; and all this would pass
into mist, even cherishable mud, the delicate

entrance of tentative leaves and the grass
renewed when the sun opened its gate.

The Renaissance, brightening, had painted altars,
ceilings, cupolas, feasts with an arched dog,

this city's painters, the guild in her ateliers
made her sublime and secular as fog.

GET DRUNK!

Paris may not be the heartland of winegrowing France, but it still has its own vine at Montmartre (celebrated more for its diuretic qualities than for its flavour – 'C'est le vin de Montmartre, / Qui en boit pinte en pisse quatre'), survivor of many more vines in the past; it's also home to the Council of the Cup-Bearers of France, a brotherhood of boozers who dress in ermine. They swear an oath 'to venerate for all time and in every place our good mother Vine, to worship her beloved son, the Wine as be his due'. Poets were not immune to the charms of wine, and American writers in Paris between the wars were notorious for their drinking (with Hemingway in the lead).

The poems in this brief hiccough of a chapter follow no logical order but stagger around joyfully with no call for formal introduction.

Get Drunk

by Charles Baudelaire (1864),
translated by Laurence Lerner

One should always be drunk. That's the one thing that matters. In order not to feel the horrible burden of Time, which breaks your shoulders and crushes you to the ground, one should be drunk without ceasing.

But on what? On wine, on poetry or on virtue, as it suits you. But get drunk.

And if sometimes, on the steps of a palace, on the green grass of a ditch, in the lonely gloom of your room, you wake up, the drunkenness already abated or completely gone, ask the wind, the wave, the star, the bird, the clock, everything that flies or groans or rolls or sings or speaks, ask everything what time it is; and the wind, the wave, the star, the bird, the clock will answer: 'Time to get drunk. In order not to be the martyred slaves of Time, get drunk. Get drunk ceaselessly. On wine, on poetry, or on virtue, as it suits you.'

The Absinthe-Drinker
by Arthur Symons (1890)

Gently I wave the visible world away.
Far off I hear a roar, afar yet near,
Far off and strange, a voice is in my ear,
And is the voice my own? the words I say
Fall strangely, like a dream, across the day;
And the dim sunshine is a dream. How clear,
New as the world to lovers' eyes, appear
The men and women passing on their way!

The world is very fair. The hours are all
Linked in a dance of mere forgetfulness.
I am at peace with God and man. O glide,
Sands of the hour-glass that I count not, fall
Serenely: scarce I feel your soft caress,
Rocked on this dreamy and indifferent tide.

Symons, a Decadent poet himself, composed this sonnet while sitting at a bar table of Aux Deux Magots on Boulevard Saint-Germain. The rhythm glides and slides, just as the speaker glides into oblivion on a wave of the drink that poets such as Baudelaire, Verlaine, Rimbaud and Wilde loved. Also known as 'la fée verte' it was thought to be addictive, cause hallucinations and even lead to blindness.

Spring in Paris
by Jim Burns (2005)

I saw him walking along the Rue Rambuteau,
and he clutched his bottle of cheap wine
as if there wouldn't be another that day.
Crowds of tourists went by, but he didn't beg,
he had his wine, enough for the time ahead,
And what he would do when it was gone
was something to be worried about later.
There was sufficient for the moment.
And just then, despite everything I knew,
and with my progress carefully planned,
I wanted to be like him, not measuring hours,
and simply concerned to catch that feeling
when a sip of wine is all that is needed
to satisfy the desire for something more.

Jim Burns is a writer and reviewer of poetry and jazz, a historian of
fifties American Beat culture.

FROM *Vendémiaire*

by Guillaume Apollinaire (from *Alcools*, 1913),
translated by Olivia McCannon

I'm drunk from drinking the whole universe
Down by the river, watching the water flow and lull the bilanders.

Listen to me I'm the gullet of Paris
I'll drink in the universe again if I want
Listen to my universal drunken songs

And the September night drew slowly to an end
The red lights of the bridges were snuffed out in the Seine
The stars died as the day was born.

A couple of notes here: 'Vendémiaire' was the first month of the French Revolutionary calendar, October, named because it coincided with the 'vendange' or grape harvest. A 'bilander' is a two-masted merchant vessel with a trapezoidal mainsail.

FROM *The Ballad of Bouillabaisse*

by William Makepeace Thackeray (1856)

A street there is in Paris famous,
    For which no rhyme our language yields,
Rue Neuve des petits Champs its name is –
    The New Street of the Little Fields;
And there's an inn, not rich and splendid,
    But still in comfortable case –
The which in youth I oft attended,
    To eat a bowl of Bouillabaisse.

This Bouillabaisse a noble dish is —
    A sort of soup, or broth, or brew,
Or hotchpotch of all sorts of fishes,
    That Greenwich never could outdo;
Green herbs, red peppers, mussels, saffern,
    Soles, onions, garlic, roach, and dace;
All these you eat at Terrés tavern,
    In that one dish of Bouillabaisse.

Indeed, a rich and savory stew 't is;
    And true philosophers, methinks,
Who love all sorts of natural beauties,
    Should love good victuals and good drinks.
And Cordelier or Benedictine
    Might gladly, sure, his lot embrace,
Nor find a fast-day too afflicting,
    Which served him up a Bouillabaisse.

I wonder if the house still there is?
    Yes, here the lamp is as before;
The smiling, red-cheeked écaillère is
    Still opening oysters at the door.
Is Terré still alive and able?
    I recollect his droll grimace;
He'd come and smile before your table,
    And hop'd you lik'd your Bouillabaisse.

We enter; nothing's changed or older.
    'How's Monsieur Terré, waiter, pray?'
The waiter stares and shrugs his shoulder; —
    'Monsieur is dead this many a day.'
'It is the lot of saint and sinner.
    So honest Terré's run his race!'
'What will Monsieur require for dinner?'
    'Say, do you still cook Bouillabaisse?'

'Oh, oui, Monsieur,'s the waiter's answer;
   'Quel vin Monsieur désire-t-il?'
'Tell me a good one.' 'That I can, sir;
   The Chambertin with yellow seal.'
'So Terré's gone,' I say and sink in
   My old accustom'd corner-place;
'He's done with feasting and with drinking,
   With Burgundy and Bouillabaisse.'

More musings over a dinner in Paris, this time from the poet Paul
Muldoon, who grew up in Moy, Northern Ireland:

Paris
by Paul Muldoon (1977)

A table for two will scarcely seat
The pair of us! All the people we have been
Are here as guests, strategically deployed
As to who will go best with whom.
A convent girl, a crashing bore, the couple

Who aren't quite all they seem.
A last shrimp curls and winces on your plate
Like an embryo. 'Is that a little overdone?'
And these country faces at the window
That were once our own. They study the menu,

Smile faintly, and are gone.
Chicken Marengo! It's a far cry from the Moy.
'There's no such person as St Christopher,
Father Talbot gave it out at Mass.
Same as there's no such place as Limbo.'

The world's less simple for being travelled,
Though. In each fresh, neutral place
Where our differences might have been settled
There were men sitting down to talk of peace
Who began with the shape of the table.

Napoleon named this chicken dish Marengo, after his victory at the Battle of Marengo. His chef concocted it from chicken, crayfish and tomato sauce. (He also gave the name Marengo to his strongest horse.)

Sanies II
by Samuel Beckett

there was a happy land
the American Bar
in Rue Mouffetard
there were red eggs there
I have a dirty I say henorrhoids
coming from the bath
the steam the delight the sherbet
the chagrin of the old skinnymalinks
slouching happy body
loose in my stinking old suit
sailing slouching up to Puvis the gauntlet of tulips
lash lash me with yaller tulips I will let down
my stinking old trousers
my love she sewed up the pockets alive the live-oh
　　she did she said that was better
spotless then within the brown rags gliding
frescoward free up the fjord of dyed eggs and thongbells
I disappear don't you know into the local

the mackerel are at billiards there they are crying the scores
the Barfrau makes a big impression with her mighty bottom
Dante and blissful Beatrice are there
prior to Vita Nuova
the balls splash no luck comrade
Gracieuse is there Belle-Belle down the drain
booted Percinet with his cobalt jowl
they are necking gobble-gobble
suck is not suck that alters
lo Alighieri has got off au revoir to all that
I break down quite in a titter of despite
hark
upon the saloon a terrible hush
a shiver convulses Madame de la Motte
it courses it peals down her collops
the great bottom foams into stillness
quick quick the cavaletto supplejacks for mumbo-jumbo
vivas puellas mortui incurrrrrsant boves
oh subito subito ere she recover the cang bamboo for bastinado
a bitter moon fessade à la mode
oh Becky spare me I have done thee no wrong spare me
    damn thee
spare me good Becky
call off thine adders Becky I will compensate thee in full
Lord have mercy upon us
Christ have mercy upon us

Lord have mercy upon us

The title is Latin for 'morbid discharge', and the poem follows the
form of a Provençal dirge or lament.

DEFIANCE, REBELLION AND REVOLUTION

Paris has always been a breeding ground for revolution and protest, and it was often through poetry that dissidence found its voice, a way round oppression and a flowering of expression. Cocteau commented, 'Poetry always causes a scandal. It is a stroke of luck that nobody notices it. It only becomes visible, alas, a long time afterwards, when events imitate it and disturb the world.'

FROM *The Poet*
by Stewart Home

The Poet is a very fierce creature. It is first cousin to the gorilla. It insults emperors, kings, princes, presidents, prime ministers, likewise members of their families. It has long, unkempt hair on its head and all over its face. Instead of fingernails it has long, sharp claws. The Poet has many pockets in which it carries pens, pencils, pads, notebooks, French cigarettes and slim volumes of verse. It is a night animal. After dark, it gathers in groups, large and small, on the pavements outside cafés, where it plans readings and character assassinations in both prose and rhyme. Lots are drawn to select those who must carry out the work.

The Poet does not like water. It never washes or changes it clothes. It is always thirsty and drinks wine and spirits. The home of the Poet is in Russia or France, especially Paris. Some few have been imported to England where they are feared and hated by all decent folks, and hunted wherever they go.

Stewart Home was born in London in 1962. He describes himself as a 'rampant plagiarist bent on reinventing world culture in its entirety'.

The rebel poet of Paris *par excellence* was of course François Villon, the father of the *poètes maudits*. He was born in Paris in 1431, the year Joan of Arc was burnt at the stake. He completed a Master of Arts in Theology in 1452. Three years later he was jailed at the Grand-Châtelet for knifing a priest in the groin in a street brawl and thereby killing him; after six months he was released.

In 1456 Villon published his *Lais* or *Le Petit Testament* and was banished from Paris for taking part in a robbery at his old college. He was then imprisoned for theft in the castle of Meung-sur-Loire, where he wrote *Le Grant Testament*. He returned to Paris in 1461 and was arrested the following year and convicted of murder (again in a brawl). He was sentenced to death by hanging; while awaiting execution with other prisoners, he composed the following ballad, about which the nineteenth-century French poet Théophile Gautier wrote, 'It will be seen that he cared little enough whether or not he was made into an earring for Mistress Gibbett.'

The Ballade of the Hanged
by François Villon,
translated by Algernon Charles Swinburne

Men, brother men, that after us yet live,
    Let not your hearts too hard against us be;
For if some pity of us poor men ye give,
    The sooner God shall take of you pity.
    Here are we five or six strung up, you see,
And here the flesh that all too well we fed
Bit by bit eaten and rotten, rent and shred,
    And we the bones grow dust and ash withal;

Let no man laugh at us discomforted,
    But pray to God that He forgive us all.

If we call on you, brothers, to forgive,
    Ye should not hold our prayer in scorn, though we
Were slain by law; ye know that all alive
    Have not wit alway to walk righteously;
    Make therefore intercession heartily
With Him that of a Virgin's womb was bred,
That His grace be not as a dry well-head
    For us, nor let Hell's thunder on us fall;
We are dead, let no man harry or vex us dead,
    But pray to God that He forgive us all.

The rain has washed and laundered us all five,
    And the sun dried and blackened; yea, perdie,
Ravens and pies with beaks that rend and rive
    Have dug our eyes out, and plucked off for fee
    Our beards and eyebrows; never are we free,
Not once, to rest; but here and there still sped,
Drive at its wild will by the wind's change led,
    More pecked of birds than fruits on garden-wall:
Men, for God's love, let no gibe here be said,
    But pray to God that he forgive us all.

Envoy

Prince Jesus, that of all art Lord and Head,
Keep us, that Hell be not our bitter bed;
    We have nought to do in such a master's hall.
Be not ye therefore of our fellowhead,
    But pray to God that He forgive us all.

On appeal, Villon's death sentence was commuted to ten years of exile. He vanished from record in 1463 when he left Paris. Twenty-six years later the first printed edition of his *Grant Testatment* was published in Paris. Villon would not have seen this as it's assumed he had died by 1489 at the latest. There is a statue of him in Square Paul-Langevin.

In homage to Villon, Swinburne wrote a ballad of his own in 1877, clearly inspired by a close reading of Villon's own ones.

A Ballad of François Villon, Prince of all Ballad-Makers

by Algernon Charles Swinburne

Bird of the bitter bright grey golden morn
Scarce risen upon the dusk of dolorous years,
First of us all and sweetest singer born
Whose far shrill note the world of new men hears
Cleave the cold shuddering shade as twilight clears;
When song new-born put off the old world's attire
And felt its tune on her changed lips expire,
Writ foremost on the roll of them that came
Fresh girt for service of the latter lyre,
Villon, our sad bad glad mad brother's name!

Alas the joy, the sorrow, and the scorn,
That clothed thy life with hopes and sins and fears,
And gave thee stones for bread and tares for corn
And plume-plucked gaol-birds for thy starveling peers
Till death clipt close their flight with shameful shears;
Till shifts came short and loves were hard to hire,

When lilt of song nor twitch of twangling wire
Could buy thee bread or kisses; when light fame
Spurned like a ball and haled through brake and briar,
Villon, our sad bad glad mad brother's name!

Poor splendid wings so frayed and soiled and torn!
Poor kind wild eyes so dashed with light quick tears!
Poor perfect voice, most blithe when most forlorn,
That rings athwart the sea whence no man steers
Like joy-bells crossed with death-bells in our ears!
What far delight has cooled the fierce desire
That like some ravenous bird was strong to tire
On that frail flesh and soul consumed with flame,
But left more sweet than roses to respire,
Villon, our sad bad glad mad brother's name?

Envoi

Prince of sweet songs made out of tears and fire,
A harlot was thy nurse, a God thy sire;
Shame soiled thy song, and song assoiled thy shame.
But from thy feet now death has washed the mire,
Love reads out first at head of all our quire,
Villon, our sad bad glad mad brother's name.

The pulse of Parisians beats to the rhythm of revolution, its songs run in the veins of the city's poets.

Writing the introduction to a guidebook to Paris, Victor Hugo explains the turmoils of his age:

1789: this figure has been a concern to the human race for almost a century now. The entire modern phenomenon is contained within it. […] Without 1789, the supremacy of Paris would be an enigma. For consider this: Rome has more majesty, Treves more antiquity, Venice more beauty, Naples more grace, London greater wealth. What then has Paris? The Revolution.

Paris is the city around which, on a given date, history turned on its pivot.

Palermo has Mount Etna, Paris has thinking; Constantinople is closer to the sun, Paris is closer to civilization. Athens built the Parthenon, but Paris destroyed the Bastille.

But poets who lived through the Revolution often had high hopes for it (before the Reign of Terror set in), seeing in it the key to spiritual emancipation as well the triumph over oppression. Words-worth was one of these, and William Blake wore the trademark Phrygian cap of the French revolutionaries. Wordsworth went to Paris briefly on his way to Orleans then Blois in 1790,

> a time when Europe was rejoiced,
> France standing on the top of golden hours,
> And human nature seeming born again

En route, confronting the wretched lives of the French peasantry, he was inoculated with fervent Republican opinions, and the belief that, with the overthrow of the existing Regime,

> We should see the earth
> Unthwarted in her wish to recompense
> The meek, the lowly, patient child of toil,
> All institutes for ever blotted out
> That legalised exclusion, empty pomp
> Abolished, sensual state and cruel power,
> Whether by edict of the one or few;
> And finally, as sum and crown of all,
> Should see the people having a strong hand
> In framing their own laws; whence better days
> To all mankind.

He even entertained dreams of joining the Girondist party and becoming one of their leaders. In the following extract, again from *The Prelude*, Wordsworth relates his visit to Paris in October 1792: the Champ de Mars, the Rue du Faubourg Saint-Antoine just east of Place de la Bastille and heartland of the Revolution, Montmartre ('Mont Martyr'), and the Panthéon ('the Dome of Geneviève'). Then to the Palais-Royal ('Palace of Orléans') which was royally owned and so protected from the police, and had quickly become a place of gambling and vice. There he picks up a stone left over from the destruction of the Bastille prison on 14 July 1789. The stones were used, for the most part, in the construction of Pont de la Concorde. He feels disappointed to be less moved than at the sight of a painting by the court painter to Louis XIV (now in the Louvre)!

FROM *The Prelude*
by William Wordsworth (1805)

Through Paris lay my readiest course, and there
Sojourning a few days, I visited,
In haste, each spot of old or recent fame,
The latter chiefly; from the field of Mars
Down to the suburbs of St Antony,
And from Mont Martyr southward to the Dome
Of Geneviève. In both her clamorous Halls,
The National Synod and the Jacobins,
I saw the Revolutionary Power
Toss like a ship at anchor, rocked by storms;
The Arcades I traversed, in the Palace huge
Of Orléans; coasted round and round the line
Of Tavern, Brothel, Gaming-house, and Shop,

Great rendezvous of worst and best, the walk
Of all who had a purpose, or had not;
I stared and listened, with a stranger's ears,
To Hawkers and Haranguers, hubbub wild!
And hissing Factionists with ardent eyes,
In knots, or pairs, or single. Not a look
Hope takes, or Doubt or Fear is forced to wear,
But seemed there present; and I scanned them all,
Watched every gesture uncontrollable,
Of anger, and vexation, and despite,
All side by side, and struggling face to face,
With gaiety and dissolute idleness.

Where silent zephyrs sported with the dust
Of the Bastille, I sate in the open sun,
And from the rubbish gathered up a stone,
And pocketed the relic, in the guise
Of an enthusiast; yet, in honest truth,
I looked for something that I could not find,
Affecting more emotion than I felt;
For 'tis most certain, that these various sights,
However potent their first shock, with me
Appeared to recompense the traveller's pains
Less than the painted Magdalene of Le Brun,
A beauty exquisitely wrought, with hair
Dishevelled, gleaming eyes, and rueful cheek
Pale and bedropped with everflowing tears.

FROM *The French Revolution*
by William Blake (1791)

Then the Abbé de S[i]eyes rais'd his feet
On the steps of the Louvre; like a voice of God following a storm,
    the Abbé follow'd
The pale fires of Aumont into the chamber, as a father that bows
    to his son;
Whose rich fields inheriting spread their old glory, so the voice of
    the people bowed
Before the ancient seat of the kingdom and mountains to be
    renewed.
'Hear, O Heavens of France, the voice of the people, arising from
    valley and hill,
O'erclouded with power. Hear the voice of vallies, the voice of
    meek cities,
Mourning oppressed on village and field, till the village and field
    is a waste.
For the husbandman weeps at blights of the fife, and blasting of
    trumpets consume
The souls of mild France; the pale mother nourishes her child to
    the deadly slaughter.
When the heavens were seal'd with a stone, and the terrible sun
    clos'd in an orb, and the moon
Rent from the nations, and each star appointed for watchers of
    night,
The millions of spirits immortal were bound in the ruins of
    sulphur heaven
To wander inslav'd; black, deprest in dark ignorance, kept in awe
    with the whip,
To worship terrors, bred from the blood of revenge and breath of
    desire,

In beastial forms; or more terrible men, till the dawn of our
    peaceful morning,

Till dawn, till morning, till the breaking of clouds, and swelling
    of winds, and the universal voice,

Till man raise his darken'd limbs out of the caves of night, his
    eyes and his heart

Expand: where is space? where O Sun is thy dwelling? where thy
    tent, O faint slumb'rous Moon?

Then the valleys of France shall cry to the soldier, "Throw down
    thy sword and musket,

And run and embrace the meek peasant." Her Nobles shall hear
    and shall weep, and put off

The red robe of terror, the crown of oppression, the shoes of
    contempt, and unbuckle

The girdle of war from the desolate earth; then the Priest in his
    thund'rous cloud

Shall weep, bending to earth embracing the valleys, and putting
    his hand to the plow

Shall say, "No more I curse thee; but now I will bless thee: No
    more in deadly black

Devour thy labour; nor lift up a cloud in thy heavens, O
    laborious plow,

That the wild raging millions, that wander in forests, and howl in
    law blasted wastes,

Strength madden'd with slavery, honesty, bound in the dens of
    superstition,

May sing in the village, and shout in the harvest, and woo in
    pleasant gardens

Their once savage loves, now beaming with knowledge, with
    gentle awe adorned;

And the saw, and the hammer, the chisel, the pencil, the pen,
    and the instruments

Of heavenly song sound in the wilds once forbidden, to teach the
    laborious plowman
And shepherd deliver'd from clouds of war, from pestilence, from
    night-fear, from murder,
From falling, from stifling, from hunger, from cold, from slander,
    discontent and sloth;
That walk in beasts and birds of night, driven back by the sandy
    desert
Like pestilent fogs round cities of men: and the happy earth sing
    in its course,
The mild peaceable nations be opened to heav'n, and men walk
    with their fathers in bliss."
Then hear the first voice of the morning: "Depart, O clouds of
    night, and no more
Return; be withdrawn cloudy war, troops of warriors depart, nor
    around our peaceable city
Breathe fires, but ten miles from Paris, let all be peace, nor a
    soldier be seen!" '

Robert Southey wrote in a letter to Caroline Bowles that

> Few persons but those who have lived in it can conceive or
> comprehend what the memory of the French Revolution was,
> nor what a visionary world seemed to open upon those who
> were just entering it. Old things seemed passing away, and
> nothing was dreamt of but the regeneration of the human race.

But the Revolution also brought the Terror and the guillotine.
Charged with tyranny and treason, Robespierre defended himself
to the Convention in July 1794. Coleridge and Southey dramatised
the end of his life in *The Fall of Robespierre*, written in August 1794
when they were both undergraduates, only a month after Robes-
pierre's execution.

Once more befits it that the voice of truth,
Fearless in innocence, though leagerd round
By envy and her hateful brood of hell,
Be heard amid this hall; once more befits
The patriot, whose prophetic eye so oft
Has pierced thro' faction's veil, to flash on crimes
Of deadliest import. Mouldering in the grave
Sleeps Capet's caitiff corpse; my daring hand
Levelled to earth his blood-cemented throne,
My voice declared his guilt, and stirred up France
To call for vengeance. I too dug the grave
Where sleep the Girondists, detested band!
Long with the shew of freedom they abused
Her ardent sons. Long time the well-turn'd phrase
The high fraught sentence and the lofty tone
Of declamation thunder'd in this hall,
Till reason midst a labyrinth of words
Perplex'd, in silence seem'd to yield assent.
I durst oppose. Soul of my honoured friend,
Spirit of Marat upon thee I call –
Thou know'st me faithful, know'st with what warm zeal
I urg'd the cause of justice, stripp'd the mask
From factions deadly visage, and destroy'd
Her traitor brood. Whose patriot arm hurl'd down
Hebert and Rousin, and the villain friends
Of Danton, foul apostate! those, who long
Mask'd treason's form in liberty's fair garb,
Long deluged France with blood, and durst defy
Omnipotence! but I it seems am false!
I am a traitor too! I – Robespierre!
I – at whose name the dastard despot brood
Look pale with fear, and call on saints to help them!

Who dares accuse me? who shall dare belie
My spotless name? Speak, ye accomplice band,
Of what am I accus'd? of what strange crime
Is Maximilian Robespierre accus'd,
That through this hall the buz of discontent
Should murmur? who shall speak?

The final words of the play, after Robespierre's execution, are uttered by Barrère as he sums up Robespierre and the Terror:

The last worst traitor triumphed – triumph'd long,
Secur'd by matchless villainy. By turns
Defending and deserting each accomplice
As interest prompted. In the goodly soil
Of Freedom, the foul tree of treason struck
Its deep-fix'd roots, and dropt the dews of death
On all who slumbered in its specious shade.
He wove the web of treachery. He caught
The listening crowd by his wild eloquence,
His cool ferocity that persuaded murder,
Even whilst it spake of mercy! – never, never
Shall this regenerated country wear
The despot yoke. Though myriads round assail,
And with worse fury urge this new crusade
Than savages have known; though the leagued despots
Depopulate all Europe, so to pour
The accumulated mass upon our coasts,
Sublime amid the storm shall France arise,
And like the rock amid surrounding waves
Repel the rushing ocean. – She shall wield
The thunder-bolt of vengeance – she shall blast
The despot's pride, and liberate the world!

Marie Antoinette

by Heinrich Heine, from *Romancero* (1851),
translated by Edgar Alfred Bowring

The plate-glass windows gleam in the sun
　　In the Tuileries Castle gaily;
And yet the well-known spectres of old
　　Still walk about in it daily.

Queen Marie Antoinette still doth haunt
　　The famous pavilion of Flora;
With strict etiquette she holds her court
　　At each return of Aurora.

Full dress'd are the ladies, – they most of them stand,
　　On tabourets others are sitting,
With dresses of satin and gold brocade,
　　Hung with lace and jewels befitting.

Their waists are small, their hoop-petticoats swell,
　　And from underneath them are peeping
Their high-heel'd feet, that so pretty appear, –
　　If their heads were but still in their keeping!

Not one of the number a head has on,
　　The queen herself in that article
Is wanting, and so Her Majesty boasts
　　Of frizzling not one particle.

Yes, she with the toupée as high as a tower,
　　In dignity so resplendent,
Maria Theresa's daughter fair,
　　The German Caesar's descendant,

She, curlless and headless, now must walk
    Amongst her maids of honour,
Who, equally headless and void of curls,
    Are humbly waiting upon her.

All this from the French Revolution has sprung,
    And its doctrines so pernicious,
From Jean Jacques Rousseau and the guillotine,
    And Voltaire the malicious.

Yet strange though it be, I shrewdly think
    That none of these hapless creatures
Have ever observed how dead they are,
    How devoid of head and features.

The first *dame d'atour* a linen shift brings,
    And makes a reverence lowly;
The second hands it to the queen,
    And both retire then slowly.

The third and fourth ladies curtsy and kneel
    Before the queen discreetly,
That they may be able to draw on
    Her Majesty's stockings neatly.

A maid of honour curtsying brings.
    Her Majesty's robe for the morning;
Another with curtsies her petticoat holds
    And assists at the queen's adorning.

The mistress of the robes with her fan
    Stands by, the time beguiling;
And as her head is unhappily gone,
    With her other end she is smiling.

> The sun his inquisitive glances throws
>> Inside the draperied casement;
> But when the apparitions he sees,
>> He starts in fearful amazement.

Heinrich Heine was born in Düsseldorf not long after the French Revolution in 1797 and grew up under French occupation of the Rhineland. He was beloved of composers of *lieder* such as Schumann, Schubert and Liszt, and there exist over 3,000 settings of his poems to music. He was a fervent supporter of the French ideals of the Revolution and a critic of the aristocracy in his native country, and spent much of his adult life in Paris. He wrote to a friend in Germany,

> If anyone asks you how I'm getting on here, tell them: 'Like a fish in water.' Or, rather, tell them that when one fish asks another fish how he's getting on, the reply is, 'Like Heine in Paris.'

He died in 1856 and was buried in the Montmartre cemetery.

On 4 September 1870, after the surrender of Napoleon III to the Prussians in the Franco-Prussian war, a republic was proclaimed. The next day Victor Hugo crossed the French border and travelled to Paris in triumph. But the year was to be one of horrors. The disgrace of the army's defeat in the Franco-Prussian war was followed by a four-month German siege of Paris, during which the citizens ate sawdust bread, dogs, cats and rats. On 13 March 1871 Hugo's son Charles died; two months later the Commune was suppressed in a week of street fighting, shelling, fires and violence – the 'Semaine Sanglante' – with many survivors summarily executed. Up to 25,000 Parisians were killed by their fellow-countrymen, a further 20,000 sent to prison or camps in French Guiana. In the next poem Hugo refers to the year 1870.

On a Barricade

from *The Terrible Year* by Victor Hugo,
translated by Henry Carrington

Upon a barricade, across the streets,
Where blood of criminal and hero meets,
Ta'en with the men, a child of twelve or less!
'Were you one of them – you?' The boy said 'Yes.'
'Well,' said the officer, 'then you'll be shot;
Wait for your turn.' The child saw the spot
All his companions 'neath the wall fall low.
To the officer he cried, 'Sir, let me go,
And take this watch to mother, who's at home.'
'You wish to 'scape,' – 'No! I'll come back.' – 'This scum
Are cowards. – Where do you live?' – 'There, by the well;
And, Captain, I'll return – the truth I tell.' –
'Be off, young scamp.' The child ran off, and then
At the plain trick laughed officer and men. –
Death's rattle mingling with their laugh was heard;
But the laugh ceased when suddenly appeared
The child, with bloodless cheek but dauntless eye,
And, leaning 'gainst the wall, said, 'Here am I!'
Death fled ashamed. – The Captain said 'Be free.

Child! – I know not in storms, where mingled be
All things right, wrong, knave, hero – in this fray,
What made you take a part; – But this I say,
Your soul, untaught, was yet sublimely great,
Good, brave – who in the very jaws of fate,
First to your mother walked – then to the grave!
Children have candour – men remorse may have.
No fault of yours to march where others led

But noble, valiant thou! who chose instead
Of safety, life, spring, dawn, and boyish play,
The black blank wall where slain thy comrades lay.'

Following the 'Semaine Sanglante', Rimbaud – whom Albert Camus described as 'the poet of revolt, and the greatest of them all' – wrote this satire of the French bourgeoisie who'd sought refuge at Versailles during the siege and then returned to Paris as great victors:

The Parisian Orgy or Paris Repopulated
by Arthur Rimbaud,
translated by Olivia McCannon

O cowards, look at her! Pour from the stations!
With blazing lungs the sun scorched clean
The boulevards the Barbarians overran that night.
Look at the Holy City where she sits in the West!

Go! We won't let the fires flare up any more,
There are the quays! There the boulevards! There,
Shimmering over the rooftops, the pale azure,
Turned red that night with starbursts of bombs.

Hide dead palaces in the cracks between planks!
The alarm of the old day brightens your faces.
Here come that redheaded troop grinding their hips,
Rage, you'll be their fools, with your rolling eyes!

Mish-mash of poultice-eating bitches on heat. The call
Of gilded houses lures you back. Steal!
Eat! The night of deep-spasmed joy has come
And spills out into the street, o desolate drinkers,

Drink. When the light comes, bright and wild,
Searching the flood of luxuries by your side,
Don't just drool into your glasses, lost for words,
For a sign, your staring eyes in a distant fog,

But swallow, for the Queen's cascading buttocks!
Listen to the creak of those inane, tearing hiccups.
Listen to those groaning idiots, old men, lackeys, puppets
Humping and screwing their way through burning nights.

O hearts of filth, unspeakable mouths,
Work harder, work, stinking lips! Bring wine
And toast these foul torpors, on these altars . . .
Your bellies are wasted with shame, o Conquerors!

Open your nostrils to these magnificent nausea!
Tip powerful poisons down your throats!
Laying folded hands on your childlike napes
The Poet says to you: o cowards – Rage!

As you grope your way through Woman's guts,
You fear she'll suffer another convulsion
And screaming, smother your infamous litter
Against her breast, in a terrible grip.

Syphilitics, kings, puppets, ventriloquists, lunatics,
Why would Paris – the whore – give a fig
For your bodies and souls, your poisons and rags?
She'll shake you off, bunch of loud-mouthed crooks!

When you're down and out, clutching your stomach,
Deadbeat, desperate, clamouring for your money,
Far from your stupor, the red courtesan,
Her breasts big with battle, will shake busy fists!

To think that your feet drummed their furious dance,
Paris! To think you were stabbed over and over,
To think that you lay dying, your faint pupils barely
Reflecting the kindness of the stained red spring,

O aching city, o city more dead than alive,
Your head and breasts thrusting into the Future
Whose million doors open onto your pallor,
City that only the sombre Past might bless:

Your magnetized body braced for the troubles,
You drink of this horrible life once more! You feel
Its flow of livid worms turn in your veins,
Its icy fingers prowl your pallid love!

And it's no bad thing. Your worms, your livid worms
Can no more stop your breath of Progress than
The Strix could peck out the eyes of the Caryatides
Where tears of astral gold fell from the blue degrees.

Although it pains us to see you under this cloud:
Although a city has never been made more
Of a stinking ulcer on verdant Nature,
The Poet says to you: 'Splendid is your Beauty!'

The storm has hailed you as supreme poetry;
The massive stirring of forces is your succour;
Your handiwork boils, death seethes, chosen City!
Muster your stridors at the bugle's muted heart.

The Poet will imbibe the sobbing of the inglorious,
The loathing of the drudges, the clamouring of the Cursed;
And the rays of his love will castigate the Women.
His stanzas will rant: Look, you crooks, look!

– Society, all is restored – the orgies wail
Their age-old ululation in age-old brothels and dives:
And delirious gases, on the red city walls,
Blaze and loom up against the pale azure sky!

May 1871

Born in the Ardennes in 1854, Arthur Rimbaud was publishing poems in respected journals while still at school and reading Victor Hugo, Théodore de Banville, Leconte de Lisle and the Parnassians, for whom 'Only that which serves no end is beautiful; everything useful is ugly.' Stifled by his overbearing and pious mother and by the straitjacket of small-town Charleville, he escaped to Paris to seek out the poets he admired. Verlaine helped him with his train fare after Rimbaud had written to admire his *Fêtes galantes* poems and to send him poems of his own, including 'Le Bateau Ivre', whose genius immediately astonished Verlaine. Soon a passionate affair exploded between them, sowing disruption in its wake. Verlaine abandoned his wife and baby, and the whole family – and society – were scandalised. Rimbaud and Verlaine wrote, advised each other (Rimbaud often leading Verlaine to more experimental verse, despite being his junior by ten years), drank to excess, travelled to Belgium and London. In 1873 Verlaine talked of attempting a reconciliation with his wife and Rimbaud of returning home to Charleville. In one of his accesses of despair and violence, Verlaine fired two shots at Rimbaud, hitting him in the wrist. He was sentenced to two years in jail.

Rimbaud considered the poet as a seer, a visionary. He willed himself to hallucinate, to reach the heightened state where such vision was possible. 'The Poet makes himself a seer by a long, immense and reasoned derangement of all the senses.' He went beyond the boundaries of the verse of his time, wanted to reinvent language, give it colour and heightened meaning. According to the poet Paul Valéry, 'Before Rimbaud all literature was written in the language of common sense.' He expanded the possibilities of language, gave it greater energy and meaning through inspired experimentation.

Rimbaud wrote all his poetry by the age of nineteen, prose a year or two later. After that he travelled: Vienna, Java, Holland, Sweden, Egypt and Abyssinia. He had been a teacher of French in England, a seller of key-rings in the streets of Paris, had unloaded vessels in ports and helped to gather in the harvest in the country. He enlisted in the Dutch army in 1876; 1878 saw him working as a foreman in a quarry in Cyprus. Then Aden, where he worked for an export company, travelling to Somalia and Gala, trading in coffee, perfumes, ivory, gold, even guns. After an infection to his knee which amputation didn't stop, he returned to Charleville and then died in 1891. It was Verlaine who had Rimbaud's works published posthumously and who fought to gain him recognition.

Villon and students of medieval times set a precedent which would continue down the generations of Rive Gauche students. Slogans, songs and verses of rebellion, cries of dissent and revolt created a cacophony to accompany the student revolts of 1968. Among them was the war cry 'La poésie est dans la rue'; or 'The barricade blocks the street but opens the way' as once more Paris streets were barricaded. One poem ran:

> If I think that nothing should change, I am a dickhead.
> If I do not want to think, I am a coward.
> If I think it is in my interest that nothing changes,
>   I am a bastard.
> If I am a dickhead, a coward and a bastard . . . I am
>   for de Gaulle.

Early on during the events of May 1968, students taunted the Right by singing 'The Internationale' under the Arc de Triomphe, and this symbolic act enraged them more than anything else that had gone before then, triggering a violent crackdown on the students and other demonstrators. ('The Internationale' is itself of Parisian birth, composed by the great freedom fighter Eugène Pottier under the Commune.)

SURREALISM, WAR, OCCUPATION

The twenties spawned Surrealism, in a post-war climate of experimentation and revolution. World War II decimated many of the artists of Montparnasse but the Surrealists found a powerful platform for their voice, radicalising many as they had to go underground during the German occupation of Paris in 1940. They revived interest in Lautréamont and Rimbaud and took inspiration from Baudelaire. They were based at their 'bureau de recherches surréalistes, 15 rue de Grenelle' and included artists such as Max Ernst, Magritte, de Chirico, Man Ray, Salvador Dalí, and the writers Antonin Artaud, Benjamen Péret, Paul Éluard, Robert Desnos, Philippe Soupault and Pierre Reverdy. They sought to unveil the truths hidden in the subconscious, often as revealed in dreams. They organised collective hypnotic sessions and wrote 'spontaneously' (*l'écriture automatique*).

The movement's leader was André Breton, who had worked in a neurological centre during the war then visited Freud and translated his works into French. He set out in his manifesto of 1924 the following definitions for the term Surrealism:

Dictionary: Surrealism, n. Pure psychic automatism, by which one proposes to express, either verbally, in writing, or by any other manner, the real functioning of thought. Dictation of thought in the absence of all control exercised by reason, outside of all aesthetic and moral preoccupation.

Encyclopedia: Surrealism. Philosophy. Surrealism is based on the belief in the superior reality of certain forms of previously neglected associations, in the omnipotence of dream, in the disinterested play of thought. It tends to ruin once and for all other psychic mechanisms and to substitute itself for them in solving all the principal problems of life.

Breton and Soupault are also credited with inventing automatic writing: prose texts with no obvious narrative, characters, action or plan that flow automatically from their pens, as if dictated by the subconscious.

For Breton, the Surrealist image was created thus: 'To compare two subjects as distant as possible one from the other, or, by any other method, to bring them face to face, remains the highest task to which poetry can aspire.' Or 'a chance encounter between two distant realities'.

Meanwhile, Louis Aragon described Surrealism in his *Paris Peasant* of 1926:

I announce to the world this momentous news item: a new vice has just been born, man has acquired one more source of vertigo – *Surrealism*, offspring of frenzy and darkness. Walk up, walk up, this is the entrance to the realms of the instantaneous, the world of snapshot. ... The vice named *Surrealism* is the immoderate and impassioned use of the stupefacient *image*, or rather of the uncontrolled provocation of the image for its own sake and for the element of unpredictable perturbation and of metamorphosis which it introduces into the domain of representation: for each image on each occasion forces you to revise the entire Universe. And for each man there awaits discovery a particular image capable of annihilating the entire Universe. You who begin to glimpse the orange gleams of this charm, hurry, bring your lips up to this cool, burning cup.

As Nadeau, a historian of Surrealism, aptly put it, 'You can't write about Surrealism, you can't paint it, you must live it.' And they did: they trashed smart apartments at banquets, hurled abuse at bourgeois bores, broke out in brawls, stole each other's lovers and generally lived it up. They set up new headquarters in a small workshop in Rue du Château in Montparnasse where poets and artists alike would eat, listen to music, read poetry and play games, when they weren't at one of the cafés they made famous – La Closerie des Lilas, la Rotonde, Le Sélect, Le Dôme and La Coupole.

The Surrealist movement broke up by 1930 amid a welter of quarrels and reconciliations, disputes over the nature of aesthetics and political commitment. Robert Desnos left in 1927; Paul Éluard abandoned the Surrealist mode of writing in favour of celebrating life in the real world; Aragon became a hard-line supporter of anti-Trotskyist Marxism. The following poems by Desnos and Éluard date from after their ruptures with the Surrealist movement.

Rue Saint-Martin Couplets
by Robert Desnos (1942),
translated by Olivia McCannon

I've gone off the Rue Saint-Martin
Since André Platane went away.
I've gone off the Rue Saint-Martin,
I've gone off wine, off everything.

I've gone off the Rue Saint-Martin
Since André Platane went away.
He was my friend, my mate.
We shared a room and a plate.
I've gone off the Rue Saint-Martin.

He was my friend, my mate.
He disappeared one day,

No one knows how or why, they took him away.
We never saw him again in the Rue Saint-Martin.

No point in imploring the saints,
Merri, Jacques, Gervais and Martin,
Not even Valérien tucked up on the hill.
Time goes by and still we know nothing.
André Platane has left the Rue Saint-Martin.

Robert Desnos (1900–1945) was a journalist, radio reporter, film writer. In 1920 he served with the army in Morocco and on his return to Paris joined the Surrealists. He became known for his ability to fall asleep under hypnosis. Louis Aragon wrote:

> At the café in the hubbub of voices, in plain daylight, and the elbowing, Robert Desnos has only to shut his eyes, and he speaks, and in the midst of the bocks, the saucers, the whole place collapses with a prophetic roar . . . Let those who question the formidable sleeper merely give him a nudge and immediately prophecy, the voice of magic, of revelation, of Revolution, the tone of the fanatic and the apostle rises to the surface.

According to another eye-witness, though, a doctor sometimes had to be called to wake him from this semi-lethargy. In this state of wakeful sleeping he would write at great speed, then rearrange his words once he was awake, thereby composing his poems. (Just before he died he confessed that his somnambulism had all been faked.)

Desnos broke with the Communist Party and later the Surrealists after failing to encourage Communists and Surrealists to work together and bring about a revolution.

During the war he was active in Resistance, meeting Nazis and passing their news on to his contacts, and writing poems and newspaper articles directly to oppose the right-wing collaborators.

A year after the publication of this poem he was arrested and deported. He died of typhus at the Terezin concentration camp shortly after its liberation.

The Last Poem
by Robert Desnos (1945)

I have dreamt so very much of you
I have walked so much, talked so much,
Loved your shadow so much,
That nothing more is left to me of you.
All that is left to me is to be a shadow among shadows
To be a hundred times more of a shadow than the shadow
To be the shadow that will come and come again into
                                        your sunny life.

Paris has paid homage to Desnos in the memorial next to Notre Dame, where his words are the first you read. The last sentence from the poem 'I've dreamed so much of you' is inscribed on the wall of the Monument to the Martyrs of Deportation behind the cathedral. Éluard pronounced a tribute on the return of his ashes to France: 'La poésie de Desnos, c'est la poésie du courage.'

Courage
by Paul Éluard (1943),
translated by Olivia McCannon

Paris is hungry Paris is cold
Paris no longer eats chestnuts in the road
Paris is dressed in an old woman's old clothes
Paris sleeps standing up in the airless metro
Yet more hardship thrust on the poor

And the wisdom and the folly
Of Paris in adversity
Is the pure air is the fire
Is the beauty is the bounty
Of its starving workers
Don't cry for help Paris
You are alive with unparalleled life
And behind the nakedness
Of your pallor your gauntness
All that is human shows in your eyes
Paris my beautiful city
Slender as a needle strong as a sword
Artless and wise
You cannot bear injustice
For you the only chaos
You will break free Paris
Paris flickering like a star
Our sole surviving hope

You will break free of the weariness and mud
Brothers take heart
Those of us without helmets

Boots gloves or manners
A spark is lit in our veins
Our light returns to us

The best of us have died for us
And now their blood flows back into our hearts
And it's morning again a morning in Paris
The drawn sword of deliverance
The arena of the budding spring

Brute force has the lower hand
These slaves our enemies
If they have understood
If they can understand
They will rise up.

Paul Éluard (1895–1952) was born Eugène Grindel in 1895 in the working-class suburb of Saint-Denis, not far from the extra-ordinary basilica of the same name, burial ground of the kings and queens of France. He was called up in 1914 and reacted in horror to the war, but chose to mark his defiance through silence, much as Breton and Aragon had: 'Let us not talk of war. It is through words that it is kept alive.' Like Breton and Aragon, he joined the Dadaist movement led by Tristan Tzara after the war, a clear mark of this break from convention and bourgeois literary values. By 1929 he had moved on to the Surrealists, and soon became the most published poet of the group. In 1924 he lived in a *ménage à trois* with his wife Gala and Max Ernst in Eaubonne near Paris, until Gala left for Salavador Dali. He outgrew the restrictions of Surrealism and in 1938 broke with Breton.

Éluard joined the underground Resistance movement during the German occupation and helped to print and circulate leaflets. 'Courage' first appeared on 14 July 1943, 'day of oppressed freedom', in an anthology of Resistance poetry, *L'Honneur des poètes*. This, according to Éluard's unsigned introduction, was poetry 'challenged to combat', which 'shouts, accuses, hopes'.

Éluard attracted the attention of the Gestapo in 1942 with his collection *Poésie et Vérité*; his poem 'Liberté, j'écris ton nom' was smuggled out of the country and printed by the British War Ministry to be dropped by RAF parachutes over France as part of a propaganda campaign. He spent the rest of the war on the run, changing his address every month, even passing himself off as an inmate of an asylum for the insane.

Cocteau wrote, 'Éluard's pure water reflects the nature of his soul and lovingly distorts it. Those who imitate it can only reflect a reflection.'

Dream
by Paul Éluard,
translated by Olivia McCannon

Dawn
I head back

The Eiffel Tower is crooked
The bridges twisted
The signs all bent

In my ruined house
My home
Not one book left

I undress.

Paris

by Louis Aragon (1944),
translated by Olivia McCannon

Where it's fair in the eye of the storm
Where it's light at the dark heart of night
Where air is strong liquor and troubles morale
Where hope still glimmers on broken tiles
And songs rise up from the rubble of walls

Blazing and rising up out of its embers
The nation's fireship keeps on burning
From Point-du-Jour to Père Lachaise
A sweet August rose in its second flowering
This, oh people, is the lifeblood of Paris.

Nothing has the sparkle of Paris ignited
Nothing's so pure as her rebel raised head
Nothing so strong – not fire, not thunder –
As Paris thumbing her nose at danger
Nothing so beautiful as this Paris of mine

Nothing will make my heart beat as fast
Nothing make me laugh so loud and weep
As my countrymen's joyful victory shout
Nothing so fine as a shroud ripped to shreds
Paris, Paris liberated, Paris, herself.

Louis Aragon (1897–1982) was mobilised in 1917 and met André
Breton while studying military medicine. Together with the poet
Philippe Soupault, they founded the review *Littérature*. Aragon
began writing, becoming an early enthusiast of Dadaism, then of
Surrealism. He was called up in World War II and took part in the

French retreat from Belgium to the Loire. His pseudonym when he was in the Resistance was François la Colère, and he published a number of poems that stirred up the anguish and humiliation of the French.

Besides the Surrealists, World War II and the occupation of Paris inspired poets and artists such as Supervielle.

Paris
by Jules Supervielle,
from *Poèmes de la France Malheureuse, Poèmes 1939–1945*,
translated by Olivia McCannon

O Paris, city opened up
Like a fresh wound
You've come a long way
From your green fields.

You are surveyed
By enemy eyes
New ears listen in
To our old noises.

The Seine is looked down on
As if from the top of a well
And night and day her
Waters flow in custody.

So many French centuries
Wrapped up in the stone
They'll walk out on us soon
In some towering rage.

The shadows are dense with faces
From foreign lands.
In the thick of such danger
Some wonder or other fades

Wanting to stay secret
Preferring to disappear
Rather than betray us
By remaining unchanged

Jules Supervielle was born of French parents in 1884 in Monte-
video, Uruguay, where he lived until the age of 10, riding over the
pampas, herding up the cattle. (Coincidentally, Lautréamont and
Laforgue were also born in Montevideo.) He then went to school
and university in Paris, and had early literary associations with
Gide, Valéry, Rivière and Rilke. He died in 1960.

Memory of France
by Paul Celan, translated by Michael Hamburger

Together with me recall: the sky of Paris, that giant
          autumn crocus . . .
We went shopping for hearts at the flower girl's booth:
they were blue and they opened up in the water.
It began to rain in our room,
and our neighbour came in. Monsieur Le Songe, a lean
          little man.
We played cards, I lost the irises of my eyes;
you lent me your hair, I lost it, he struck us down.
He left by the door, the rain followed him out.
We were dead and were able to breathe.

Paul Celan (1920–1970) was taken to labour camps in Romania in 1942, being released only in 1944, when he wrote his *Todesfuge* or 'Death fugue', a poem based on accounts of camps in Poland.

Going back in time to close this section, here is e. e. cummings, an American in Paris during World War I and a frequent visitor to the city thereafter.

16 heures
by e. e. cummings (1926)

16 heures
l'Etoile

the communists have fine Eyes

some are young some old none
look alike the flics rush
batter the crowd sprawls collapses
singing knocked down trampled the kicked by
flics rush (the

Flics, tidiyum, are
very tidiyum reassuringly similar,
they all have very tidiyum
mustaches, and very
tidiyum chins, and just above their
very tidiyum ears their
very tidiyum necks begin)
                              let us add

that there are 50(fifty) flics for every
one(1)communist and
all the flics are very organically
arranged

and their nucleus(composed
of captains in freshly-creased
-uniforms with only-just-
shined buttons
tidiyum
before and behind)has a nucleolus:

the Prefect of Police

(a dapper derbied
creature, swaggers daintily
twiddling
his tiny cane
and, mazurkas about tweak-
ing his wing collar pecking at his im
-peccable cravat directing being
shooting his cuffs
saluted everywhere saluting
reviewing processions of minions
tappingpeopleontheback

'allezcirculez')

—my   he's brave . . . .
the
communists pick
up themselves friends
& their hats legs &

arms brush dirt coats
smile looking hands
spit blood teeth

the Communists have (very) fine eyes
(which stroll hither and thither through the
evening in bruised narrow questioning faces)

DEATH AND CEMETERIES

Morgues used to loom large in the imaginations and lives of Parisians. Indeed, the Paris morgue was a tourist attraction in the late nineteenth century. Workers would gawp at the corpses in their lunch hour, the Thomas Cook tour of the city included a stop at the morgue – visitors came by their thousands every day (a million a year, according to a contemporary newspaper). A French guidebook of 1867 lists all the causes of death and the numbers of bodies over the past years, many of which were aborted foetuses and newborn babies. The morgue was closed to the public in 1907.

Apparent Failure
by Robert Browning (1864)

We shall soon lose a celebrated building.

Paris Newspaper

No, for I'll save it! Seven years since
   I passed through Paris, stopped a day
To see the baptism of your Prince;
   Saw, made my bow, and went my way:
Walking the heat and headache off,
   I took the Seine-side, you surmise,
Thought of the Congress, Gortschakoff,
   Cavour's appeal and Buol's replies,
So sauntered till – what met my eyes?

Only the Doric little Morgue!
   The dead-house where you show your drowned:

Petrarch's Vaucluse makes proud the Sorgue,
　Your Morgue has made the Seine renowned.
One pays one's debt in such a case;
　I plucked up heart and entered, – stalked,
Keeping a tolerable face
　Compared with some whose cheeks were chalked:
Let them! No Briton's to be baulked!

First came the silent gazers; next,
　A screen of glass, we're thankful for;
Last, the sight's self, the sermon's text,
　The three men who did most abhor
Their life in Paris yesterday,
　So killed themselves: and now, enthroned
Each on his copper couch, they lay
　Fronting me, waiting to be owned.
I thought, and think, their sin's atoned.

Poor men, God made, and all for that!
　The reverence struck me; o'er each head
Religiously was hung its hat,
　Each coat dripped by the owner's bed,
Sacred from touch: each had his berth,
　His bounds, his proper place of rest,
Who last night tenanted on earth
　Some arch, where twelve such slept abreast, –
Unless the plain asphalt seemed best.

How did it happen, my poor boy?
　You wanted to be Buonaparte
And have the Tuileries for toy,
　And could not, so it broke your heart?
You, old one by his side, I judge,
　Were, red as blood, a socialist,

A leveller! Does the Empire grudge
   You've gained what no Republic missed?
Be quiet, and unclench your fist!

And this – why, he was red in vain,
Or black, – poor fellow that is blue!
What fancy was it turned your brain?
Oh, women were the prize for you!
Money gets women, cards and dice
   Get money, and ill-luck gets just
The copper couch and one clear nice
   Cool squirt of water o'er your bust,
The right thing to extinguish lust!

It's wiser being good than bad;
   It's safer being meek than fierce:
It's fitter being sane than mad.
   My own hope is, a sun will pierce
The thickest cloud earth ever stretched;
   That, after Last, returns the First,
Though a wide compass round be fetched;
   That what began best, can't end worst,
Nor what God blessed once, prove accurst.

Another morbid attraction – which you can still visit – is the catacombs, accessible at Place Denfert-Rochereau. They form part of a vast network of underground tunnels that mirror the city above the surface, left over from the days when there were many mines and stone quarries in the city. They were created when the city finally decided to stop burying its dead in the overcrowded parish church cemeteries and mass graves, prompted by the collapse of the Cimetière des Innocents due to pressure from overcrowding: bodies were spewed into an adjacent apartment block.

Catacombs, Paris

by David Constantine,
from *Something for the Ghosts* (2002)

Collecting the photos at the counter next to where
She bought the testing kit he sees what he has done,
She has, they have, down there
In the deepest circle by the font that one
Script called the Samaritan Woman's Well
And the other Lethe. She is displayed
Much like a nude against the knobby wall
Of end-on femurs and humeri, arms wide
Along a dado curve of skulls. Boudoir
Or chapel apse in a kraal of bone of some
Few hundred of several millions of dead,
His lens, the flash, her look of centre spread.
The place? Down there. And when? The morning after
One of his several million sperm went home.

David Constantine has won numerous awards for fiction, translation and poetry, and is co-editor of *Modern Poetry in Translation*.

The catacombs were an interim measure before the creation of new cemeteries beyond the city centre: Montmartre, Père Lachaise, Passy in the early nineteenth century, and Montparnasse a little later.

The cemetery of Montmartre was once an abandoned limestone quarry, used as a dumping ground for victims of the Revolution, and consecrated as a cemetery in 1825. Stendhal was the first famous writer to be buried here (1842); poets include Alfred de Vigny, Théophile Gautier and Heinrich Heine. Dancers, composers and novelists keep them company in the Montmartre *quartier* which had once been the home of many artists (Renoir, Van Gogh, Utrillo, Picasso).

Towards the end of his life, Heine had a dream about the Montmartre cemetery:

> It was a bright and early morning and I was walking in the cemetery at Montmartre, where I propose to be buried one day – it's quiet and you're not disturbed nearly so much as you are at Père Lachaise. The tombstones were gleaming in the rising sun, and lo! in front of every tombstone stood a pair of highly polished shoes, women's or men's, according to whether the sleepers down below were married women, spinsters, or men. It was like a big hotel where the bootblack goes from door to door as soon as it is light and neatly and carefully places the footwear where it belongs. All the occupants of the grave were still fast asleep, but there was a magnificent shine on the polished boots, as if they had been polished by angels, and the whole picture seemed to say, 'Yes, we shall rise again and begin a new life.'

Matthew Arnold (1822–1888) wrote an elegy on Heine's grave, after he visited it in September 1858; it begins:

> '*Henri Heine*' – 'tis here!
> That black tombstone, the name

Carved there – no more! and the smooth,
Swarded alleys, the limes
Touched with yellow by hot
Summer, but under them still,
In September's bright afternoon,
Shadow, and verdure, and cool.
Trim Montmartre! the faint
Murmur of Paris outside;
Crisp everlasting-flowers,
Yellow and black, on the graves.

Half blind, palsied, in pain,
Hither to come, from the streets'
Uproar, surely not loth
Wast thou, Heine! to lie
Quiet, to ask for closed
Shutters, and darkened room,
And cool drinks, and an eased
Posture, and opium, no more;
Hither to come, and to sleep
Under the wings of Renown.
Ah! not little, when pain
Is most quelling, and man
Easily quelled, and the fine
Temper of genius so soon
Thrills at each smart, is the praise,
Not to have yielded to pain!
No small boast, for a weak
Son of mankind, to the earth
Pinned by the thunder, to rear
His bolt-scathed front to the stars;
And, undaunted, retort

> 'Gainst thick-crashing, insane,
> Tyrannous tempests of bale,
> Arrowy lightnings of soul.

To give the Père Lachaise more prestige and encourage its use after it was built in 1804, the remains of Molière and La Fontaine, and then Héloïse and Abélard were reburied there. More recently, poets buried in the Lachaise include Alfred de Musset, Béranger, Villiers de L'Isle-Adam, Gérard de Nerval, Henri de Régnier, Guillaume Apollinaire and Paul Éluard. Also Oscar Wilde, Colette, Victor Hugo and Chopin.

Apollinaire's tombstone often has fresh roses laid on it. It is inscribed with a heart which reads 'My Heart the same as a flame upside down' and with the following lines from *Calligrammes* (1918), translated by Oliver Bernard:

> At last I have become detached
> From every single natural thing
> Now I can die but cannot sin
> And what no one has ever touched
> I have touched and felt it too
> I have examined everything
> That no one can at all imagine
> I have weighed and weighed again
> Even imponderable life
> I can die and smile as well

The Death of Guillaume Apollinaire

by Tristan Tzara,
translated by Lee Harwood

we know nothing
we knew nothing of grief
the bitter season of cold
carves long scares in our muscles
he would have sooner loved the joy of victory
wise with quiet sadnesses   caged
can do nothing

if snow fell upwards
if the sun rose here during the night
to warm us
and the trees hung with their wreath
– the only tear –
if the birds were among us to be reflected
in the quiet lake above our heads
ONE WOULD UNDERSTAND
death would be a fine long journey
and limitless holidays for flesh structures and bones

Tristan Tzara (1896–1963) founded the Dada movement with Hans Arp and Richard Huelsenbeck in Zurich in 1917, naming it by opening the dictionary at random. It fell open at the word 'dada', meaning hobby-horse according to some, the tail of an African cow according to others, nothing at all according to Tzara himself. The movement revolted against established writers and values, defied respectable society, opposed war and rejected convention.

After the war the Dadaists met in Paris. Followers included Breton, Aragon, Soupault and Éluard; the artists Juan Gris, Ribemont-Dessaignes, de Chirico, Léger, Picabia, the musicians

Satie, Auric, Milhaud, Poulenc, Clicquet. In 1924 Breton broke from the Dada group and founded the Surrealist group, writing its manifesto.

Tzara admired Apollinaire above all other poets, as he embodied the qualities of lucidity, simplicity, immediacy, entirety, necessity. He praised the bareness of Apollinaire's poetry, 'the exact, real, totally unpromiscuous nudity of the word which is only itself, intended in its round force, with no background of allusions, or, rather, with none of the seductions of sublimated imagery'.

The Montparnasse cemetery opened in 1824. Poets buried there include Baudelaire, the Parnassian poets Théodore de Banville, François Coppée, Leconte de Lisle and Catulle Mendès; Robert Desnos, Léon-Paul Fargue (*Piéton de Paris*), César Vallejo, Tristan Tzara – and Serge Gainsbourg, whom François Mitterrand called 'our Baudelaire, our Apollinaire'. The cemetery is home to many other writers too: Samuel Beckett, Jean-Paul Sartre, Simone de Beauvoir, Joris-Karl Huysmans, François Mauriac, Marguerite Duras, Eugène Ionesco, Julio Cortázar, Joseph Kessel, Sainte-Beuve, Barbey d'Aurevilly and Maupassant.

The Tomb of Charles Baudelaire
by Stéphane Mallarmé,
translated by Ciaran Carson

Through the slimy open grating of a storm-drain
The entombed temple slobbers muck and rubies,
Abominable as the dog-god Anubis,
Whose muzzle blazes with a howl of savage pain.

It's like the new gas of an odorous campaign
Against the dark, illuminating our disease –
Immortal whore as old as Mephistopheles,
Who flits from lamp to lamp beside the foggy Seine.

What wreaths, in cities of no votive evenings,
Can offer benediction to us, as she flings
Herself in vain against a marble Baudelaire?

As trembling veils of light absent her from our gaze,
She has become his deadly-nightshade-poisoned air,
That we must breathe, although we perish in its maze.

Stéphane Mallarmé (1842–1898), the acknowledged leader of the
Symbolists, held a salon every Tuesday evening when living in
Paris and teaching English at the prestigious Lycée Condorcet:
Verlaine, Leconte de Lisle, Maeterlinck, Zola, Huysmans, Mau-
passant would meet, along with fledgling writers André Gide, Paul
Claudel and Paul Valéry, and visitors including Henry James,
George Moore, Oscar Wilde and Algernon Swinburne.

Black Stone upon a White Stone

by César Vallejo, from *Poemas humanos* (1939),
translated by Eugenio Florit

I shall die in Paris at a time of heavy showers,
on a day of which I already possess the memory.
I shall die in Paris – and I'm not dismayed –
perhaps on a Thursday, like today, in the autumn.

It shall be a Thursday, because today, Thursday, as I prose
these lines, my forearms ache badly,
and, never before, in all my life,
have I felt myself so lonely as today.

César Vallejo is dead; everybody kept hitting him
even though he has done nothing to them;
they hit him hard with a stick, and hard,

also, with a rope; his witnesses are
the Thursdays and the bones of his arms,
the loneliness, the rain, the roads . . .

The title of the poem recalls the ancient practice of memorialising a happy event with a white stone, an unfortunate one with a black stone. The Peruvian poet César Vallejo moved to Paris in 1923 after he'd been imprisoned in Peru for a feud he'd not been involved in and for being an 'intellectual instigator'. He'd already published two volumes of poetry and continued to write in Paris, and went on to form the Peruvian Socialist Party. He died shortly after visiting Spain and witnessing the civil war, which shocked him deeply. His remains are in the Montparnasse cemetery.

Paris

by Louise Michel,
translated by Olivia McCannon

Nothing but shadow spilling from its dark urns;
Nothing but this gloomy night, its speechless ghosts;
The water lies forbidding and still, and in its deep bed,
A chasm held open, a mystery waiting, immense,
In the grim silence, you suddenly hear
Something drop from a bridge.

At once, it's as if the pale streetlamps,
As if every breath that poverty ever froze,
As if the living dead and the cold departed,
The crooks lurking in the shadows of doors
All converge on the morgue, where, uncounted,
They disappear as they step in.

A hideous procession! Men, women, terrified
Children, some bodies, others souls, endlessly,
For all they might protest, pass on, pass on,
All are there! As ghosts, or maybe thoughts, yes,
All have a place, and come morning, their passing
Shows its gaping, sorry trace.

Paris, 1861

Ten years after writing this poem, Louise Michel, a schoolteacher in Montmartre, was to rise to fame as the passionate 'Red Virgin', the Joan of Arc of the Siege of Paris and Commune. She led the Women's Vigilance Committee and proclaimed during the siege, 'Here in Paris, we breathe an odour of death. Treason is rampant.

We must not let the people sleep. Let us be on our guard.' When court-martialled for her Communard activities she appeared in the dock in black, threw back her veil and said, 'If you are not cowards, kill me. If you let me live, I shall never cease to cry for vengeance.' She was deported to New Caledonia and lived until 1905.

PARIS AFTER DUSK

Clichés about Paris abound, among them the notion of the 'City of Light', perhaps born of visitors' dreams of glittery evenings in cabarets and bars. The term 'city of light' was originally in fact used in homage to Paris when it was the intellectual centre of the Enlightenment, and later because it was one of the first cities to have electric street lighting.

Baudelaire wrote of twilight Paris, and the evil and decay lurking in the shadows. Unlike other poets who sought refuge from the growing pollution of the city or ignored the chasm between wealthy and poor – retreating to nature or into themselves – Baudelaire cast an unflinching gaze on the harsh realities of the city. He drew unsentimental inspiration from filth, carrion, sexual deviation, nightmare.

Evening Twilight
by Charles Baudelaire,
translated by Laurence Lerner

Evening has come, the burglar's friend, at last,
With all its charms. The sky grows overcast
Like a low ceiling as the light grows dim.
Man turns to wolf as darkness closes in.

Evening, the happy hour, longed for by those
Whose aching muscles only need repose
After an honest day's hard work. Relief
To those devoured by unrelenting grief:

the plodding scholar with his aching head,
The crippled workman crawling to his bed.
But noxious demons too wake up again,
Slowly and sluggishly, like business men;
They knock against the shutters as they pass.
The wind torments the lamps and through the glass
The twisted shapes grow brighter, and then fade.
The streets light up with lust; the girls parade.
The antheap opens: down long corridors
The spies of lust crawl, mumbling with their jaws,
Through mud, to undermine the helpless town
 – Armies of worms, that filch their food from man.

Each evening kitchens whistle; here and there
Theatres yelp, orchestras start to snore;
The cafés where we gamble and eat chips
Fill up with half-clad girls with painted lips,
Their ponces, muggers, thieves, who only see
What's in your pocket; gently, skilfully,
Force open doors and safes: on what they take
They and their moll can manage for a week.

Soul, stop and think a moment. Let the roar
Drift past, and shut your ears; this is the hour
When invalids get worse, when sombre Night
Grabs at their throat, and into the common pit
With them. That ward is full; and more than one
Will never sit and eat his soup again
Next to his hearth while his beloved wife
Looks on and watches
                                    – to say nothing of
Those who've had nothing of domestic life.

Morning Twilight

by Charles Baudelaire,
translated by Laurence Lerner

Morning. The bugle sounds. The streetlamps shake
In the dawn wind. Slowly the houses wake.

A swarm of nightmares twisting their dark heads,
The adolescents disarrange their beds.
Throbbing and turning like a Cyclops' eye
My lamp is a red stain upon the day.
The soul beneath its weight of blood and bone
Enacts that conflict of the lamp and dawn.
The air is damp, with tears upon its skin;
It trembles; the breeze dries its face.
                                      A man
Throws down his pen; the woman turns her back,
Saying, 'Enough'. The chimneys start to smoke.
Stupid with sex, the whores upon their beds
Drop off to sleep, pale-eyed, with aching heads.
A beggar woman pokes the dying brands,
Rubs her thin breasts, and blows upon her hands.

Women in labour close their eyes in pain;
Their screams redouble as the day is born.
Like a consumptive sobbing in his chest
A cock crows somewhere, tearing at the mist.

The roofs are islands in a ghostly sea.
This is death's moment. Unremittingly
He walks the wards for victims, and they choke.
Young men in evening dress stroll through the park
Or step from taxis, tired with the night's work.

Dawn shivers as it slinks across the Seine,
Wearing its dressing-gown of pink and green,
And Paris, poor old horse, blinks its tired eyes,
Feeling the harness tighten on its flesh.

FROM *Maldoror*

by Lautréamont,
translated by Paul Knight

The shops of the Rue Vivienne display their riches to wondering eyes. Lit by numerous gas-lamps, the mahogany caskets and gold watches shed showers of dazzling light through the windows. Eight o'clock has struck by the clock of the Bourse: it is not late! Scarcely has the last stroke of the gong been heard than the street, the name of which has already been mentioned, starts to tremble, and is shaken to its foundations from the Place Royale to the Boulevard Montmartre. Those who are out walking quicken their steps and thoughtfully retire to their houses. A woman faints and falls on the pavement. Nobody helps her up; everyone is anxious to get away from those parts . . . [...] Now in that place which my pen (that true friend, who acts as my accomplice) has just shrouded in mystery, if you look in the direction where the Rue Colbert turns into the Rue Vivienne, you will see, in the angle formed by the intersection of these two streets, the profile of a character moving with light footsteps towards the boulevards. But if you come closer, in such a way as not to attract the attention of this passer-by, you will observe with pleasant surprise that he is young! From a distance one would in fact have taken him for a mature man. The total number of days no longer counts when it is a matter of appreciating the intellectual capacity of a serious face. I am an expert at judging age from the physiognomic lines of the brow: he is sixteen years and four months of age. He is as handsome as the retractility of the claws in birds of prey; or, again, as the unpredictability of muscular movement in sores in the soft part of the posterior cervical region or, rather, as the perpetual motion rat-trap which is always reset by the trapped animal and which can go on catching rodents indefinitely and works even when it is hidden under straw; and, above all, as the chance juxta-position of a sewing machine and an umbrella on a dissecting table!

Lautréamont, born Isodore Ducasse, wrote the epic prose poem *Les Chants de Maldoror* in 1868 at 15 Rue Vivienne. It represents an act of defiance, a revolt against the Romantic sentimentality of Alfred de Musset, Lamartine and others. It breaks with the con-ventions of poetry that were so carefully set out by Malherbe in the sixteenth century and followed thereafter, and sets out to redraw the rules of poetry and hit the reader hard with a new form of poetics, new imagery, new sources of inspiration. André Breton called him 'le grand serrurier de la vie moderne', the great lock-smith or unlocker of modern life.

Lautréamont died in a hotel during the Prussian siege of Paris in December 1870, aged twenty-four, reasons unknown, on a day when dog meat was selling at 2.50 francs a pound and cat meat 12 francs.

Kiss Me

by Jacques Prévert, translated by Sarah Lawson

It was in a district of the City of Light
Where it's always dark where there's never any air
In winter and summer it's always winter there
She was on the stair
He was beside her she was beside him
It was night
It smelled of sulphur
Because they'd been killing bedbugs that afternoon
And she said to him
It's dark here
There's no air
Winter and summer it's always winter
God's sun doesn't shine our way
It has far too much to do in the rich neighbourhoods
Hold me in your arms
Kiss me
Kiss me for a long time
Kiss me
Later it will be too late
Our life is now
Here everything kills you
The heat and the cold
You freeze you suffocate
You can't get any air
If you stopped kissing me
I think I would suffocate
You're fifteen and I'm fifteen
So we're thirty together
At thirty you're not children any more

You're old enough to work
And old enough to kiss each other
Later it will be too late
Our life is now
Kiss me!

The Noise of Cabarets
by Paul Verlaine,
translated by Dorothy Brown Aspinwall

The noise of cabarets, the filthy thoroughfare,
The weary plane-trees shedding leaves in the night air
The bus, a hurricane of iron, mud, and ooze
That sways on its unstable wheels, and creaks, and whose
Red and green eyes from side to side it slowly rolls.
The workmen bound for clubs are flaunting the clay bowls
Of short, mouth-burning pipes beneath the nose of cops.
Slippery cobbles, seeping walls, dripping rooftops,
Bumpy asphalt with drainage that does not suffice,
My customary route – that leads to paradise.

Paul Verlaine was born in Metz in 1844 and moved to Paris with his family as a boy. By the age of fourteen he had read Baudelaire's *Les Fleurs du Mal* in secret and sent Victor Hugo a poem of his own. He soon began to drink and was found a civil servant job at the Hôtel de Ville by his father. He continued his life of dissipation and his writing regardless. In 1868 he published eight poems in an edition of *Parnasse contemporain* alongside poems by Leconte de Lisle, François Coppée and Stéphane Mallarmé. He married in 1870, at least as much to qualify for a married man's deferment from the Franco-Prussian war which had just broken out as for love of his young wife Mathilde. In 1871 he received some poems from an unknown poet of seventeen and invited him to Paris. So it was he met Arthur Rimbaud, and introduced him to Paris, its poets, and the hallucinatory drink of absinthe. Rimbaud in turn seduced the older poet at least as much as he was seduced, and the pair would be lovers, quarrel and be reunited, until Verlaine was sent to prison for shooting Rimbaud in the wrist during a drunken altercation. After prison he wrote *Sagesse* and attempted to reform, but he continued to drink. He found fame as a poet in later years and went to great efforts to publish and celebrate the works of Rimbaud. His own poetry was lyrical, musical, sometimes pious, at other times pornographic, always passionate. He died in 1896.

Sketches of Paris

by Paul Verlaine, from *Etchings*, in *Poèmes Saturniens* (1866),
translated by Olivia McCannon

> The moon plated its shades of zinc
> At obtuse angles.
> Tails of smoke like coiling fives
> Rose thick and black from high sharp roofs.
>
> The sky was grey. The North Wind sobbed
> Like a bassoon.
> Far off, a cold wan tom-cat
> Mewed in a strange shrill tone.
>
> I kept walking, dreaming of the divine Plato
> And of Phidias
> Of Marathon and Salamis
> Beneath blinking rows of blue gas eyes.

In Paris

by Marina Tsvetaeva,
translated by Sasha Dugdale

Roofs reach the stars, the sky is low,
And closer to the earth, its vapours thronging
In Paris, so large, so full of joy,
Still the old secret longing.

The evening boulevards hum and throb
The last light of dusk dies.
Everywhere couples, couples in love,
Trembling lips and brazen eyes.

I'm alone here. How sweet
To lean my head on a chestnut's bole
And hear in my heart Rostand weep
As he did once before, in Moscow.

Paris at night is strange and piteous –
Dearer to my heart is the fevered past
I go home, to the violets' dreariness
And a tender face behind picture glass.

That gaze – companion to my sorrow
That fond profile on the wall,
Rostand, and Reichstadt, his poor hero
And Sarah, at night they visit me, all.

In Paris, so large, so full of joy
I see grass, I see high clouds in my sleep
And laughter far off, and shadows close by
And the pain is always just as deep.

Marina Tsvetaeva (1892–1941) studied at the Sorbonne in 1908, then returned to live in Paris for fourteeen years in 1925, exiled from the Soviet Union. She was not assimilated into the society of fellow Russian émigrés; she sided with poets who were still in Soviet Russia and thereby became unpopular in Paris. In a letter of 1927 she wrote, 'In Paris, with rare exceptions, everyone hates me; they write all sorts of nasty things, leave me out in all sorts of ways, and so on.' But this early poem dates from the time when Tsvetaeva studied alone in the city, and not her later years of exile. Pasternak wrote of her,

> Tsvetaeva's early manner . . . was exactly what all the Symbolists, from first to last, dreamed of and did not achieve. And while they spluttered helplessly in their linguistic ocean of lifeless schemes and dead archaic forms, Tsvetaeva soared over the real difficulties of creation, solving its problems effortlessly and with matchless technical skill.

Rostand, author of *Cyrano de Bergerac*, wrote a play called *L'Aiglon* about the sad fate of Napoleon I's son, the Duke of Reichstadt. Sarah Bernhardt later acted this role in Paris. Tsvetaeva translated *L'Aiglon* into Russian in her teens.

Paris

by Ingeborg Bachmann, from *Mortgaged Time*,
translated by Mark Anderson

Lashed to the wheel of night,
the lost ones sleep
down below, in the thundering tunnels –
but where we are, there is light.

Our arms are laden with flowers,
mimosa from many years.
Gold falls from bridge to bridge,
breathless in the river.

Cold is the light,
colder still the stone before the gate;
and all the fountain basins
are half drained.

What will happen if we stay here,
homesick to the root of our flowing hair,
and ask: what will happen
if we survive beauty's trial?

Lifted high on the wagon of light,
though waking, we are lost
in the streets of genius, above –
but where we are not, there is night.

The Austrian poet and dramatist Ingeborg Bachmann said in an interview in 1964, 'I am not overly fond of poetry and don't read it willingy. In my reading, poems take up a very small space.'

In the World's Heart: Found Fragment
by Blaise Cendrars, translated by Anselm Hollo

This Paris sky, cleaner than winter sky lucid with cold –
I've never seen nights more starry, more bushy, than this spring
With boulevard trees like shadows of heaven,
Great fronds in rivers choked with elephant ears,
Heavy chestnuts, leaves of plane trees –

White water lily on the Seine, moon held by water's thread,
Milky Way in the sky flops down on Paris, embraces
The city, crazy, naked, upside down, mouth sucking Notre Dame.
Great Bear and Little Bear prowl around Saint-Merry, growling.
My cut-off hand shines in the skies – in Orion.

In this hard cold light, trembling, more than unreal,
Paris is like the frozen image of a plant
That reappears in its ashes. A sad simulacrum.
Linear, ageless, the buildings and streets are only
Stone and steel, heaped up, an unlikely desert.

Babylon, Thebes, no more dead tonight than the dead city of Paris
Blue, green, inky, pitchy, its bones bleached in starlight.
Not a sound. Not a footfall. The heavy silence of war.
Eye pans from pissoirs to violet eye of streetlights:
The only lit space into which I can drag my restlessness.

And that's the way I walk Paris each night,
From Batignolles to the Quartier Latin, crossing the Andes
Under the lights of new stars, greater, more puzzling:
Southern Cross more prodigious, each step one takes toward it
    as it emerges from the old world
Above the new continent.

I'm the one who has run out of past. Only my stump still hurts me.
I've rented a hotel room to be alone with myself.
A brand-new wicker basket to fill up with manuscripts.
No books, no pictures, no knick-knacks to please me.

Desk cluttered with newsprint,
I work in this empty room, behind a blind window,
Bare feet on red congoleum, play with balloons, a child's
       trumpet. I work on THE END OF THE WORLD.

Cendrars here describes wartime Paris at dead of night. During World War I he was sent to the front, and in 1915 he lost his right arm and was discharged from the army. This is from a radio interview with Michel Manoll in 1950:

CENDRARS: In 1917 I had just written a poem which astounded me by its fullness, its modernity, by everything I'd put into it. It was so antipoetic! I was delighted. And at that moment I decided not to publish it, to let modern poetry get along without me, to see what would happen to it. I nailed this unpublished poem in a chest; I put the chest in an attic in the country, and I set myself a limit of ten years before I'd take it out to publish it. That's more than thirty years ago, and I believe the time has not yet come to publish it.

INTERVIEWER: This poem is 'Au Cœur du Monde' ['In the world's heart']?

CENDRARS: Yes, and although unpublished, it's famous. The other day an editor offered me a million for it, but I didn't bite.

    I told you the other day that I don't write any more poems. I make poems which I recite to myself, which I taste, which I play with. I feel no need to communicate them to anyone, even to people I like a lot. I don't write them down. It's so good to daydream, to stammer around something which remains a secret for oneself. It's a sin of gluttony.

THE LEAVES OF PARIS

Paris's parks and green spaces seem immutable, a constant even through times of turmoil and change. The statues in the Jardin du Luxembourg weather the snows and rains, the children's boats sail across the pond, the trees continue to be pollarded every spring – all creates a counterbalance to the artificial paradises of the city's most decadent poets.

Elizabeth Barrett Browning and Robert Browning spent 1855–1856 in a flat on Rue du Colisée. This extract from Barrett Browning's *Aurora Leigh* shows Paris manicured into exuberant flowering by design: the trees as much as the fountains the flourishing of art and design.

> A serious riddle: find such anywhere
> Except in France; and when it's found in France,
> Be sure to read it rightly. So, I mused
> Up and down, up and down, the terraced streets,
> The glittering Boulevards, the white colonnades
> Of fair fantastic Paris who wears boughs
> Like plumes, as if a man made them, – tossing up
> Her fountains in the sunshine from the squares,
> As dice i' the game of beauty, sure to win;
> Or as she blew the down-balls of her dreams,
> And only waited for their falling back,
> To breathe up more, and count her festive hours.
>
> The city swims in verdure, beautiful
> As Venice on the waters, the sea-swan.
> What bosky gardens, dropped in close-walled courts,

As plums in ladies' laps, who start and laugh:
What miles of streets that run on after trees,
Still carrying the necessary shops,
Those open caskets, with the jewels seen!
And trade is art, and art's philosophy,
In Paris.

A Path in the Luxembourg

by Gérard de Nerval (1834),
translated by Olivia McCannon

She passed me by, that young lady
Lithe and lively as a bird:
In her hand a shimmering bloom,
On her lips the freshest tune.

Might it be she of all in the world
Whose heart alone might answer mine,
Who'd venture into my dark night
And with one look, fill it with light!

But no, my youth has been and gone . . .
Farewell sweet beam that on me shone, –
Scent, young lady, harmony...
Joy passed me by, – escaping me!

The Merry-Go-Round
by Rainer Maria Rilke,
translated by Stephen Cohn

Jardin du Luxembourg

The team of painted ponies spins around
against the shadow of the canopy,
part of the ancient brightly coloured land
which stays and clings and ends reluctantly;
and some draw little carriages behind
but all of them look mettlesome and strong.
A small white elephant goes sailing by,
the fierce red lion follows him along.
A stag as real as in some woodland scene
although it wears a saddle: on it rides
a tiny girl in blue, strapped safely in.

A small white elephant goes sailing by,
the lion bears a little boy in white,
the fearsome creature shows its teeth and glares,
the hot excited hands hold very tight.

And so they ride and so they circle round
and round again, and lively girls are there
for whom such games are practically outgrown
whose eyes look everywhere, search everywhere.

A small white elephant goes sailing by
and all continues hastening towards an end,
circling and circling round and finding none;
a red horse, and a green, a grey and then
a little face, unfinished, just begun.

And sometimes children's voices unrestrained
sound out in brilliant laughter, while they stay
enchanted in their breathless, endless, play.

Rilke's wife Clara Westhoff was a pupil of Rodin and passed on to Rilke her reverence for the master; when in 1902 he was commissioned to write a book on him, he left Germany and went to Paris. He worked with Rodin for less than a year before they fell out, but he stayed in Paris, on and off, until 1911. He was reconciled with Rodin when he showed him the Hôtel Biron on Rue de Varenne (now the Musée Rodin). Built for a wealthy wigmaker, the house was acquired in 1904 by the French government and given over to artists' studios. When Clara Westhoff returned to Germany Rilke moved into her studio and worked on the *Notebooks of Malte Laurids Brigge* there. He thought Rodin would like the vast main gallery and suggested it to him.

Rilke's Paris is sometimes one of terror, neurosis. He began *The Notebooks of Malte Laurids Brigge* with the line 'So this is where people come to live; I would have thought it is a city to die in.' He wrote in a letter of 1903,

In August of last year I arrived there. It was the time when the trees in the city are withered without autumn, when the burning streets, expanded by the heat, will not end and one goes through smells as through many sad rooms . . . When I passed by the Hôtel Dieu for the first time, an open carriage was just driving in, in which a person hung, swaying with every movement, askew like a broken marionette, and with a bad sore on his long, grey, dangling neck. And what people I met after that, almost every day; fragments of caryatids on whom the whole pain still lay, the entire structure of a pain, under which they were living slow as tortoises. And they were passers-by among passers-by, left alone and undisturbed by fate . . . And they were wearing the comfortless, decoloured mimicry of the too great cities, and were holding out under the foot of each day that trod on them, like tough beetles, were enduring as if they still had to wait for something, twitching like bits of a big chopped-up fish that is already rotting but still alive.

Nevertheless, Rilke's Paris years were fertile ones, producing the third part of *The Book of Hours* (1907), *New Poems* (1906 and 1907) and *The Notebooks of Malte Laurids Brigge* (1910), which took him six years to complete.

The poet and film director Jean Cocteau wrote in his *Paris Album 1910–1914* that as a mere schoolboy he came across the Hôtel Biron and managed to rent a room as a secret retreat:

> One door, for which I possessed an enormous key, opened on to an archway, and the archway on to a garden. Garden, park, kitchen garden, Paradise, how can I describe it? Anyone lacking the jaundiced eye of youth would have fallen over backwards. Did Paris really live, walk, circulate, work and keep going round such a silence? For although it existed only through this contrast, the silence none the less imposed itself more firmly, suppressing the ear to the benefit of the eye, emanating from the grass and the trees, stifling the din of a city through that force of habit which makes silence a privilege of abandoned gardens. It was, if you like a spectacle of silence, a phenomenon arising from the way we nearly always look at things instead of listening. I meant that the sound of music distracts us less from looking than looking distracts us from listening; that looking at something does not prevent you from hearing music; and that the visual impression of being a thousand miles from Paris, in the middle of the country, transported you at the same time into the midst of silence.

But his mother found out about Cocteau's second home and put an abrupt end to it.

Long, long afterwards I was to know whose lamp it was that burned every night behind a corner window. It was the lamp of Auguste Rodin's secretary, Rilke. I thought I knew many things and I lived in the crass ignorance of pretentious youth. Success had put me on the wrong track and I did not know that there is a kind of success worse than failure, and a kind of failure which is worth all the success in the world. Neither did I know that the distant friendship of Rainer Maria Rilke would one day console me for having seen his lamp burn without knowing that it was signalling to me to go and singe my wings against its flame.

Jardin du Luxembourg (after Rilke)
by Derek Mahon (2006)

A merry-go-round of freshly painted horses
sprung from a childish world vividly bright
before dispersing in adult oblivion
and losing its quaint legendary light
spins in the shadows of a burbling circus.
Some draw toy coaches but remain upright;
a roebuck flashes past, a fierce red lion
and every time an elephant ivory-white.

As if down in the forest of Fontainebleau
a little girl wrapped up in royal blue
rides round on a unicorn; a valiant son
hangs on to the lion with a frantic laugh,
hot fists gripping the handles for dear life;
then that white elephant with ivory tusks –
an intense scrum of scarves and rumpled socks
though the great whirligig is just for fun.

The ring revolves until the time runs out,
squealing excitedly to the final shout
as pop-eyed children gasp there in their grey
jackets and skirts, wild bobble and beret.
Now you can study faces, different types,
the tiny features starting to take shape
with proud, heroic grins for the grown-ups,
shining and blind as if from a mad scrape.

Derek Mahon was born in Belfast in 1941 and studied French literature at Trinity College Dublin then at the Sorbonne. This poem comes from *Adaptations*, a collection of poems based on works by other poets.

Colloque Sentimental
by Paul Verlaine (1869),
translated by Arthur Symons

In the old park solitary and vast,
Over the frozen ground two forms once passed.

Their lips were languid and their eyes were dead,
And hardly could be heard the words they said.

In the old park, solitary and vast,
Two ghosts once met to summon up the past.

– Do you remember our old ecstasy?
– Why would you bring it back again to me?

– Do you still dream as you dreamed long ago?
Does your heart beat to my heart's beating? – No.

– Ah, those days, what joys have those days seen
When your lips met my lips! – It may have been.

– How blue the sky was, and our hope how light!
– Hope has flown helpless back into the night.

They walked through weeds withered and grasses dead
And only the night heard the words they said.

Mairie des Lilas

by Paul de Roux, from *À la Dérobée* (2005),
translated by Olivia McCannon

The last stop on line eleven
In a place called Lilac, is the town hall,
Pointing its chapel belfry at the sky
And tonight the sky is flooded
With spring light; in the oceanic blue
One petal still hangs, the moon,
And the vast white clouds are the steamships
Of eternity, or that's what I'll believe.
Rue du Coq-Français, Rue de Romainville
Passage des Sablons, towards Bagnolet
You find lilac and wisteria
Scaling modest suburban houses
In whose gaps infinity dresses its display.

Paul de Roux was born in Nîmes in 1937. As well as poetry he has
written a novel and a biography of the painter Henri Fantin-Latour.

An Afternoon in the Parc Monceau
by Stephen Romer (1986)

The weather was foreseen, but not the world
in its field, this was not dreamed up.
But there it was, one interwoven place
where the sun poured down and the children
were moving jewels. A poplar unfurled
its shimmering skein, the candles were dancing
in flocks on chestnut; they danced in measure,
curtsied, kept balance. And between these things
was no division.

Half way through the afternoon, a wedding came
in slow procession through the crossing place;
solemn groom, troubled bride, for all of time
stiffly on the grass. But a smiling wind
unloosed them, and blew her long veil back,
and stretched it out and worried it and showed
her face light up, so animate and lovely
her hands nor his nor any hand could tame
the joyous flapping of that veil.

Lovers on the strong breathing ground,
intercede for us, kiss and kiss, obey
the irresistible thing, be tender
as the folded bird with his soft brown eye
who shares your bank of shade, or say
one motionless branch of becoming.
Beyond them in the half-lights, benched and blessed
between columns, the old sat on amazed
as one more summer climbed to its towers.

Stephen Romer is a lecturer at the University of Tours in France. He has translated many French poets, including Paul Valéry, Philippe Jaccottet, Jean Tardieu, and Jacques Dupin. His anthology of translations, *Into the Deep Street*, co-edited and translated with Jennie Feldman, was shortlisted for the 2011 Popescu Prize.

This collection could continue and run to hundreds more pages. But lest it outgrow its pocket size, it must end, so why not with one of the earliest poems written in modern French?

Paris is Beyond Compare
by Eustache Deschamps (1370),
translated by David Curzon and Jeffrey Fiskin

When I've gone round the earth and sea
and visited all places, every one,
seen Egypt and Jerusalem and Galilee,
Damascus, Alexandria and Babylon,
Cairo and Syria and Tartary,
and entered every port,
and seen the spices and the sweets that they make there,
although they're better than the French have got,
Paris is beyond compare.

She is the city crowned above the rest,
the fount of scholarship and wisdom, and its well,
located on the river Seine, possessed
of woods and vineyards, land and dell.
She has more of the mortal good that we embrace
than any other place;

all strangers love her, will always find her fair,
because such elegance, such happiness,
will not be found in any town but this:
Paris is beyond compare.

For she's much better than any fortress town:
she has chateaux built in the days of old,
she's peopled with merchants, men of renown,
and workers of every kind, in armour, gold;
the flower of all the arts, as you've heard tell;
her workmen all excel;
deep understanding and a subtle skill
was found in her inhabitants, and is found still,
and loyalty to the craft that's in their care:
Paris is beyond compare.

Acknowledgements

Many of the translations included in this anthology are by talented poets in their own right, and their experience of translating may have contributed to their superlative mastery of verse in English too. I am especially indebted to Olivia McCannon, author of *Exactly My Own Length* (Oxford Poets), who has translated many of the French poems especially for this anthology, injecting new life and vigour into their lines. This collaboration has gone beyond enriching this collection: it's allowed the inclusion of some of the strongest, most eloquent voices of the city which would otherwise have been omitted and so left this book without the heartbeat of its great French poets.

The publishers and I would also like to thank all of the authors for making this collection possible by allowing us to use their material, and gratefully acknowledge permission to reprint copyright material as follows:

Jim Burns, for permission to use 'Spring in Paris'; New Directions Publishing Corporation for permission to use 'Trip to Paris' by Guillaume Apollinaire, translated by Roger Shattuck, from Selected Writings ©1971 by Roger Shattuck; the University of California Press for permission to use 'Sunflower' from *André Breton: Selections*, translated by Mark Polizzotti; Laurence Lerner for his permission to use his translations of Baudelaire's 'Parisian Landscape', 'Get Drunk', 'Evening Twilight', 'Morning Twilight'; Bloodaxe Books for permission to include 'Catacombs, Paris' by David Constantine, from *Collected Poems* (2004) by David Constantine; Taylor & Francis for permission to use David Curzon and Jeffrey Fiskin's translation of Eustache Deschamps' 'Paris is Beyond Compare' from *Eustache Deschamps: Collected Poems*; Les Editions de Minuit for permission

use 'Il Bacio' by Paul Verlaine, translated by Karl Kirchwey, from *Poems under Saturn* © 2011 Princeton University Press; Modern Poetry in Translation and Jane Tozer for permission to use her translation of François Villon's 'The Lament of the Gorgeous Helmet-Fettler', first published by MPT in 2011; Sasha Dugdale for permission to use her translation of Marina Tsvetaeva's 'In Paris'; Anvil Press for their permission to use Oliver Bernard's translation of 'Inscription on Apollinaire's Tombstone' taken from *Guillaume Apollinaire: Selected Poems*, published by Anvil Press Poetry in 1986 (new edition in 2004) and Peter Dale's translation of 'In the Street' by Jules Laforgue, taken from *Poems of Jules Laforgue*, published by Anvil Press Poetry in 1986 (revised edition in 2001); Faber & Faber for permission to use Samuel Beckett's poem, 'Sanies II', and his translation of 'Zone' by Guillaume Apollinaire, for permission to use an extract from 'Tiepolo's Hound' by Derek Walcott and for letting us use Paul Muldoon's poem 'Paris'.

Index of Poem Titles

Index of First Lines

Index of Poets

ELAND

61 Exmouth Market
London EC1R 4QL
info@travelbooks.co.uk
www.travelbooks.co.uk

Eland was started thirty years ago to revive great travel books which had fallen out of print. Although the list soon diversified into biography and fiction, all the titles are chosen for their interest in spirit of place. One of our readers explained that for him reading an Eland classic was like listening to an experienced anthropologist at the bar – she's let her hair down and is telling all the stories that were just too good to go into the textbook.

Five years ago we added a cheeky younger sister to our classic series, *Poetry of Place*. Intended to be opinionated and passionate, yet to fit in a pocket, these selections of poems illuminate a destination through the multiple voices of poets through the centuries. Their editors are a diverse group of poets, writers and publishers: A. N. Wilson on *England*, Anthony Thwaite on *Ruins*, John Lucas on *The Isles of Greece*, Gaia Servadio on *Tuscany and Umbria*. For a full list of all our books, including the fourteen poetry titles, please visit our website where you can order a free catalogue, or email us at our office.